9749/6/75 £3.50

||||||||||||||||||||||||||||||||||
D1825461

MOZAMBIQUE AND THE FUTURE

MOZAMBIQUE AND THE FUTURE

KERRY SWIFT

LONDON
ROBERT HALE & COMPANY

ISBN 0 7091 5081 4

First published in Great Britain 1975

ROBERT HALE & COMPANY
63 Old Brompton Road
London
SW 7   3 JU

Printed in the Republic of South Africa by Citadel Press, Lansdowne, Cape

To Sarah
whose gentle life was snuffed out before its time
and to Roy Campbell
to return the courtesy for the book
he dedicated to me.

CONTENTS

ILLUSTRATIONS

Death comes before its time
Life is so brief a stay

FERNANDO PESSOA

INTRODUCTION

There is a long-standing joke in Portuguese about the European colonial era in Africa. It concerns four men – a Belgian, an Englishman, a Frenchman and a Portuguese – who lived on the bank of a crocodile-infested river.

Each had an African servant who went down to the river each day to wash his master's underwear. One day the Belgian's servant was taken by a crocodile. The Belgian caught the first flight back to Belgium. Soon after, the Englishman's servant was taken. The Englishman took off his pith helmet, bowed his head and called for another pink-gin before the country club closed. When the Frenchman's servant vanished, the Frenchman showed great emotion, falling on to his knees on the river bank.

The next day, the Portuguese servant was grabbed at the same spot by a particularly large crocodile. The Portuguese jumped into the river, killed the reptile and dragged his servant back on to the bank where he promptly punched him in the mouth.

"That will teach you to wash my underwear where the crocodiles feed," he said.

I think, perhaps, this little story best exemplifies in its crudest terms what the Portuguese have called their "civilising mission" in Africa: Portugal alone among the European colonial powers has been prepared to swim in that river while the other colonial nations did not, instead they hid their dirty linen, forgetting who washed it in the recent past.

This book is about the Portuguese in Africa, more specifically in Mozambique, which occupies a large slice of the continent. It is a book about Portugal's war in Mozambique, but it deals too with the people who fight in that war; their thoughts and feelings.

I started to write it as a travelogue through the war, but events in Portugal and Mozambique finally dictated that it would also have political references. The military coup that ousted Dr Marcello Caetano's dictatorial Government in Lisbon on April 25, 1974, threatened to change the face of Southern Africa dramatically, and I began then to examine the events that led up to the military takeover in Portugal, how they affected Mozambique and the future of White Southern Africa.

Ultimately, the events I have described will change people's lives and, more important, their attitudes. But I have included my travelogue through Mozambique because, to my knowledge, I was the last journalist to conduct a comprehensive tour of Mozambique before the coup in Portugal and what I found there will never be the same again.

Events unfold quickly in Africa, which makes it the most exciting continent. History doesn't have to wait for the record – you can see it happening daily. And the tide of Black Nationalism that has rocked this continent to its very foundations waits for nobody. The realisation that the war in Mozambique, in fact, was a revolutionary war filtered through to the Portuguese long before it did to the White south, Rhodesia and South Africa.

The events in Portugal and Mozambique stand as a salutory lesson to the White south that historical patterns unfold with unerring regularity. Portugal's compromise to Black Nationalism in Mozambique is just another step in the tide that has swept this continent.

The recent history of Mozambique and Portugal underlines dramatically that rule with a mailed fist is in the long run self-defeating. Perhaps the Mozambique model will act as a future guideline to the White south where the value of compromise has still to be learnt.

What has to be faced is that it may still be a long time before Mozambique's agony ends, before everyone of its inhabitants learns equally to enjoy the sunshine and other benefits. Recent events could also mean that South Africa and Rhodesia will "never be the same again".

Johannesburg
September, 1974

KERRY SWIFT

CHAPTER ONE

INTO MOZAMBIQUE: LOURENCO MARQUES

"Smoke Jim?" I said holding out my last South African cigarette to James Soullier as we sat outside the Restaurante Marialva, in Lourenco Marques's Avenida da Republica one bright February morning. This restaurant is dedicated to famous bull fighters of the past and the avenue is a busy throughfare where one can watch the whole of Lourenco Marques's parade.

"Sure." He flicked his lighter across the table and smiled. James Soullier is almost everything you don't expect of an Aussie: five foot nothing, quiet spoken, retiring, and a very moderate drinker. But in other ways he qualifies – behind a camera lens he is totally fearless. What I would call reckless, he calls "a calculated risk", shrugging it off as "part of the game, cobber". But his greatest quality is his sense of humour, magnified by a warm smile that flicks across his face and lights up his ginger hair like a roman candle close to its nadir.

It was the first time we had worked together and we were still feeling each other out – he the hardened professional photographer, I the reporter at the outset of an assignment that was to take us over 8 000 km through the war-torn Portuguese province of Mozambique on the south east flank of Africa.

"Well, if these first three days are any indication of what we're up against, we may as well pack up now and go home," he said. "But I'm lucky, somehow I know we'll crack this nut and crack it well."

I wasn't so sure. Newspaper colleagues in Johannesburg had warned me of the difficulties of working in Mozambique. One in particular, a news photographer who has covered the wars in all three of Portugal's African provinces, even found it amusing. "You'll spend days waiting at airports and in musty hotel rooms – the only two words the Portuguese know in English are "not possible"; he said, and my initial overtures to Portuguese officials in South Africa were hardly encouraging.

It had all started two weeks previously in Johannesburg, in the office of Joel Mervis, editor of *The Sunday Times*, for which I worked. By any standards he is an impressive figure with a paternal air towards his staff that has an endearing if sometimes frustrating effect on one. Behind his desk in an expansive office on the sixth floor of *The Sunday Times'* Main Street building, this advocate turned newspaper Editor can be a fearsome enemy or a powerful ally.

I had been toying with the idea of covering the war in Mozambique for some time. Newspaper reports about the war were appearing with nagging regularity in the local papers and it seemed the right time to try to bring it all together for readers in South Africa, to the majority of whom Mozambique was as far removed in their thinking as Vietnam was to the average American before they suddenly found themselves fighting a war there.

Besides, I had always had a great interest in the Portuguese. This dated back to the days when my godfather, the late Roy Campbell, one of South Africa's greatest poets and authors, used to captivate me with his stories, and at times no doubt his imagination, about his romantic exploits in metropolitan Portugal. This interest crystalised when Roy was killed in a motor smash on his way back from Spain with Mary, his wife, to Sintra, his permanent home outside Lisbon.

As I walked into the Editor's office that morning, I had a feeling I had caught him in a receptive mood. I had been on leave for five weeks – perhaps there is something in absence making the heart grow fonder – and as I put my request to him, I knew he would be well disposed to the idea.

"I would like to go into Mozambique to cover the war," I said. It sounded simple enough – a statement rather than a request.

Joel Mervis looked up and peered at me through his dark-rimmed glasses.

"Why?" he said with a frown that creased his heavy features with a solemn but benign interest. Editors always demand explanations. They have to be sold on an idea – the result of many years of shooting them down and building them up. Joel Mervis, South Africa's leading editor, is no exception.

"It looks like things are hotting up there and it's the Portuguese tenth year of combat in Mozambique. I think the timing is right." I was keen to go and he must have sensed it because his final "yes, that should be in order" was meant as much as encouragement as a dismissal.

Then the problems began. Mozambique for the interested newsman is not easy to enter. Unlike the tourist playground, it is made out to be in the alluring pages of the travel brochures, Mozambique has an aura of rigid security that you sense the moment you apply for a visa.

"Have you been to Mozambique before?" the Portuguese Consul-General, Mr Carlos Almeida searched my face as he asked the question, then leaned back waiting for a reply.

"No, this will be my first visit." It seemed a strange thing to say, considering I had spent most of my life in South Africa and that the future of Southern Africa lies increasingly in war-ravaged Mozambique.

Although covert military allies, South Africa and Mozambique are like chalk and cheese – the one a strange experiment in racial segregation, the other an ambitious attempt at integration beneath the hot African sun. For many South Africans and Rhodesians, Mozambique represents a breather from the restrictive inhibitions of White supremacy – an injection of alien though not altogether unattractive culture as the many visitors to Lourenco Marques and Beira from South Africa and Rhodesia will testify by their mere presence there.

During the holiday seasons there is an exodus of tourists from the White south to Mozambique where they can lull in the shade of multi-racialism without looking over their shoulders worrying about the Joneses. Mozambique is the White south's Cuba, but like Cuba it is closing up as the guerrilla war creeps closer to the tourist haunts and the first twinges of fear ripple through the neon delights.

Mr Almeida's office, on the first floor of a run-down building in Rissik Street, Johannesburg, was in fact my first introduction to the Portuguese in any official capacity.

"You say you want to write about Mozambique. I think this can be arranged, but it will take some weeks." I had an inkling of the red tape attached to visiting the Mozambique war fronts when I phoned to make the appointment. A clipped Portuguese voice told me I would need a visa with attached photograph and a list of all the places, names and addresses of people I wished to see – no easy task for an outsider who has never been there before and has had to rely only on the snippets of information that filter through from this troubled outpost of Portuguese influence in Africa.

My informant on the phone told me my visa application would have to be cleared by DGS, the Portuguese secret police, in Lourenco Marques – more delay, but I had not expected Mr Almeida's final remark: "You should have approached the Portuguese Embassy in Pretoria, except it has been moved to Cape Town. Still, I think it can be arranged, but I shall also need clearance from Lisbon."

As I left this curt Portuguese diplomat, I wondered whether we would ever get to Lourenco Marques let alone the trouble spots in the north and central provinces where his kinsmen and their indigenous Black allies were fighting and dying for his right to issue visas.

A phone call to the Portuguese Embassy in Cape Town brought better results.

"Yes it can be arranged, but who is the photographer accompanying you?"

"James Soullier," I said.

"What passport will he be travelling on?"

"Australian." There was a distinct pause before the official said: "We aren't very well disposed to Australians, especially Australian journalists. The last one who visited Mozambique wrote a number of very damaging articles made up of fabrications. I will need an assurance that Mr Soullier will not do the same."

As a journalist it was an impossible assurance to give.

Many rumours about heavy-handed Partuguese tactics in Mozambique had come to my attention and my assignment was to search out the truth. I also had to consider allegations published in Fleet Street in which some of the London papers, notably *The Times*, accepted the story of two Spanish priests who claimed Portuguese troops had massacred the population of a village called Wiriyamu, near Tete. *The Times* had splashed the story across its front page in a great burst of journalistic conjecture that backfired when no one could substantiate the story. But still it was possible that Wiriyamu had been wiped out by the Portuguese and that there were more villages that had felt the rough end of Portuguese wrath. If the Portuguese were massacring innocent villagers, how could I give any assurances that we wouldn't expose them?

"If you are unsure, I suggest you check on our credentials. The only assurance I can give you is that we will report the war as we see it, as objectively as possible and without prejudice."

Three days later we both had twenty-day visas, a pocket full of Mozambique escudos – each Portuguese province has its own currency, a policy that has caused considerable dissatisfaction among

Portuguese subjects living in the Provinces – return tickets to the end of the line at Porto Amelia, a large bottle of vitamin pills, Maloprim to stave off malaria and a nagging dose of anti-cholera serum. Also stuck inside my baggage was a bottle of Limosin brandy.

The South African Airways Boeing 737 dipped over the harbour of Lourenco Marques, providing a panoramic view of the city with its wide boulevards and high-rise buildings. Even from the air one can sense something different about the place – a type of lazy sensuality that typifies the Latins and the Portuguese in particular.

Hugging the coast I could see the prawn and lobster boats that pepper the sea around Lourenco Marques, where, on average, they catch three to five tons of prawns a day. The larger ones, called "lagostim" or king prawns are nearly a foot long – enough to titivate the palate of the most hardened gourmet. I was not the first visitor unwittingly to order a dozen and end up in embarrassed silence with eight monster prawns untouched and the knowing frowns of the local diners falling about me with the gentle invective of all locals toward the ignorant tourist.

We were met at Lourenco Marques's airport by a busy little man wearing a safari-suit and a neatly trimmed RAF-type moustache. It was 9 a.m. and already the mid-summer heat engulfed us like a mist-lined sigh bringing everything to a slow, almost sleepy shuffle.

"You are from *The Sunday Times* . . . we have been expecting you," he said, introducing himself as Mr Gonsalves of CIT, the government tourist agency that was to act as a godsend during the later period of our trip.

We collected our baggage and were whisked through customs and immigration by our new guardian. It all seemed to be one big happy family – a smile here, a pat on the back and we were outside the airport building, where we were ushered to a waiting car while Mr Gonsalves disappeared to phone in his progress to his superiors. A few minutes later we were on our way to the hotel – discussing the bullfighting.

Later that afternoon Mr Gonsalves joined us at the Marialva, where we were enjoying a cold glass of Laurentina, the pick of Mozambique's three brands of insipid beer.

"We haven't got permission for your visit from the Governor yet, but we may as well plan your trip. What is it exactly you wish to see in Mozambique?" said Gonsalves.

"We want to bring the Portuguese war effort home to the South African public," I ventured.

"Yes, but what is it you wish to see?" We were to find that the whole concept of public relations is lost on the Portuguese. The distinction between good and bad publicity has long disappeared in a general mistrust of all foreign journalists.

I rattled off possibilities for stories, angles that might fire the imagination of my editor and the reading public in South Africa and in the countries where my articles would be syndicated. He noted them down conscientiously, adding a few suggestions of his own all so far removed from the war, I began to think we would end up doing a three-week roundup of where and how to spend our money in Mozambique for the Portuguese Government. With a curt "watch the girls and enjoy yourselves", Gonsalves left us. We weren't to hear from him again until the following day when he brought a typed itinerary, again a roundabout of the tourist sites.

I handed him a programme I had prepared the previous night. "We'll need to get permission from the secret police for that and these fall under the military in Nampula," he said as he worked his way down the list. I had cut out visits to the famous Gorongosa game reserve, Nacala and Quelimane, two natural harbours up the coast, and concentrated on the four war fronts: Cabo Delgado in the north east, Niassa in the north west, Tete province and selected areas in and around Vila Pery and the port of Beira, where guerrilla activity had become particularly marked.

Armed with the amended itinerary Gonsalves left us. It took three days to get the show on the road, get the necessary permissions from the Governor, the DGS, the army and finally to notify CIT representatives in the areas we were to visit when we would be arriving.

Our period in Lourenco Marques was not exactly wasted. It gave me the chance to speak to commercial interests about the war. Many of the local businessmen were complaining about its effect on the tourist trade on which their livelihood depends. I learned that tourism was down significantly throughout the entire territory, showing a steady decline since 1971.

Beneath the picturesque facade of life in Lourenco Marques, with the vibrant devil-may-care atmosphere, the effects of the war were beginning to show. Outside our hotel every morning we were met by former Portuguese servicemen trying to exchange Mozambique

18

escudos for South African rands. The Mozambique currency has become worthless outside the territory and a grey market of enormous proportions has sprung up in Lourenco Marques. One ex-serviceman offered me 50 escudos to the rand (the official exchange rate is about 38, although the further north in the territory you go, the less you can get for the rand.) He told me he desperately wanted to leave Mozambique, that he had the necessary permissions – they had taken nearly a year to get – but until he managed to get rid of his escudos and change them for a viable currency he was stuck in Mozambique. Similar stories were related to me throughout Mozambique.

A Scottish engineer, Jock MacLean, told me later in Nampula that the prawn boats in Lourenco Marques were in dire straits. "The engines are stuck together with string and chewing gum. There's a fortune to be made reservicing them, but I can't do a thing until they buy the spares. They can't buy spares because nobody will accept escudos," said Jock.

I met a number of people in Lourenco Marques who had sons on the war fronts. One told me her son was due to arrive home after completing his service nearly two years ago. "He is still fighting in Cabo Delgado. The last I heard of him, he was in Montepuez. Maybe he will never come home," she said looking up at a faded portrait of her son on the counter of her curio shop.

If you look critically at Lourenco Marques you can see the tarnish of war all around you: drab night-clubs peopled with painted street-walkers and off-duty soldiers on leave from the war, the occasional amputee walking like a stiff puppet on wooden army crutches and the muffled whispers in the street-side cafés about the war. There is a stoic acceptance of the war in Mozambique, but given the chance few, very few of the local White residents of Lourenco Marques, would like to fight. You cannot disguise fear in any man's eyes.

While in Lourenco Marques the Marialva became our friendly rendezvous. The visits we paid there were far removed from the reality of our assignment, but there it was, a compromise between metropolitan Portugal and Africa.

The Restaurante Marialva is a place of dreams where Portuguese can drop in and live the vicarious life of heroes for an hour while eating prawns with imported vinho verde and topping off the meal with Chiesa di Sierra and bananas.

The heroes are enshrined in the portraits round the walls – Manolete, Dos Santos, Joselito – the men who have stood in a hundred bullrings from Madrid to Mexico City, facing pedigree bulls, wicked bulls, lovely bulls, honest bulls, brave bulls and dangerous bulls. They're inscribed on the Marialva's walls. And how apt is the title – Restaurante Marialva.

In the 18th century, in Portugal, the Conde do Arcos, a young Portuguese aristocrat, was one of the attractions at a corrida where a number of good bulls were being fought. The Conde was the matador on a day when the arena was packed with joyous fans. It was a great day for this aristocratic matador – and a great day for his father, the Duke of Marialva, a dignified nobleman, white-haired and in his seventies. He was a proud man, but especially on this day as he watched the young Conde do Arcos play the bull and, eventually, prepare for the coup.

The whole stadium was tense as the kill was awaited. There was a heavy silence as the bull charged, a silence which seemed to shut in as though with a blanket of lead as the young Conde was hooked on the horns of the bull.

He died in the sunlight before the shocked gaze of the aficionados. But before the dazed crowd had begun to stir, there was a movement on the barrier. It was the Duke making his way into the arena to the body of his son. His disdain for the bull was immense.

The Duke gazed at his son and then made his way to the gaily decorated box of the President. Then, with due deference to custom, he doffed his hat, bowed to the President and formally requested permission to intrude into the fight and kill the bull.

Permission was granted and the old aristocrat took his son's sword, faced the killer bull and challenged it to charge.

When it did so his arm gained a new youthful vigour; he took aim and unerringly placed the sword in the spot over the shoulder which gave uninterrupted entry to the heart. The bull dropped dead. The Duke acknowledged the plaudits of the crowd tersely as he walked back to the body of his son. From that day the killing of bulls was forbidden in Portugal.

The bullfight is still held in Lourenco Marques today, over Easter and during the holiday seasons of July and Christmas, for the Portuguese have a great tradition of bravery typified in the bullring. But in Mozambique today the combat has been taken out of the ring and placed in the real world – the Portuguese traditions are now being tested to the limits of their endurance by a different foe, equally as well trained and equipped, but a human foe bent on the destruction of Portuguese influence in Mozambique.

CHAPTER TWO

WE HEAD NORTH: NAMPULA

The moment you leave Lourenco Marques headed north, the war becomes more evident. DETA, the nationalised Mozambique airline, flies as far north along the coast as Porto Amelia from where commercial air-taxis take over. On any regular DETA flight, it is a common sight to see dozens of troops flying back to their stations in the central and northern districts.

DETA plays an important role in the Portuguese war effort in Mozambique, transporting troops and supplies. During the Portuguese offensive, "Gordion Knot" in 1970, DETA jets played a key role in flying troops from Lourenco Marques back to the war fronts where their unexpected arrival caught Frelimo intelligence napping. But the use of commercial aircraft is not without its hazards. A cautious Army captain told me in Nampula that he would appreciate me not mentioning the name or make of any of the DETA aircraft in any of my articles.

"We don't want pressure to be brought to bear on the manufacturers in America and Germany to stop supplying spares for the DETA fleet," he said.

There is also the possibility that the use of commercial aircraft in the war effort could justify Frelimo knocking them out when they have the capability. Their use as machines of war could well blind the international community to the deaths of innocent passengers.

Nampula, the military headquarters of Mozambique, three hours drive inland from historic Mozambique Island, is one of the few spots on the African continent where the winds of change forgot to blow.

Surrounded by a circular group of surealistic mountains, Nampula looms out of the verdant bush like a forgotten mining camp; lethargic and lustreless. Its streets emit a variety of strange odours that waver from the exotic spices sought by the early Arab traders to the rank smells of decay.

Yet it has its own beauty. At sunset the surrounding bush envelops the town with its primitive calls and a sense of peace nestles down, hovering over the twilight drinkers at the street-side cafés. Nampula also acts as the military clearing house of Mozambique and as such is one of the few spots on earth where the women completely dominate the thoughts of the male community – a feature that infuriates the Latin blood which has always been partial to male chauvinism.

The town's one commercial cinema is sold out every night as frustrated Portuguese soldiers live their sexual fantasies vicariously with the Gina Lolobrigadas and Liz Taylors that infest the nightly performances and bring great gasps of appreciation from the audience.

"You have three choices in Nampula," said a despondent cinema colleague one evening. "You can pay 300 escudos at one of the brothels and a further 500 for the doctor afterwards, or there are the local girls from the school who only do it for love or you come to the cinema." I preferred the cinema and noticed my informant did as well – we saw him in the same seat every night we were there.

Another soldier told me a story that was a bit more ominous. "I took a girl out one night and the following day I was arrested by the military police. Because she was a major's daughter, I spent three days in jail. I wouldn't have minded if she was worth it, but she wasn't," he said with obvious venom.

I felt sorry for the men of Nampula. Not being great drinkers by nature, these virile Portuguese soldiers prefer to haunt the streets on the offchance of seducing the school girls or sit at the open-air cafes telling risqué stories that would knock Henry Miller's *Tropic of Capricorn* into a cocked hat. Even if they wanted to drown their sorrows in drink or take a chance with the brothels, it would have to be a rare occurrence as the average Portuguese soldier only earns R30 a month.

The women strut about with their tails in the air, leaving a trail of eager males behind them and ultimately, a host of shattered illusions. You can almost sense the process of visual defrocking that goes on. The terrible thought crossed my mind that if a female streaker wanted to cause a riot, she should parade her gifts in sex-starved Nampula.

Against the skyline surrounding Nampula one of the mountains forms a perfect silhouetted profile of a reclining African looking up at the sky. "The Old Man", as the mountain is aptly called by the locals, has a legend.

When the gilded caravels of Vasco da Gama, the great Portuguese voyager, first touched at Mozambique soil, a legendary figure known as Monomotapa, chief of the Mocarange peoples, ruled with benevolent interest over his hordes. Da Gama landed with a fierce determination to fly the Portuguese flag wherever the winds of fate should take it and his first stop was at the mouth of a river he called Rio dos Nons Sinaes (the River of Good Tokens).

After the Portuguese had established a permanent foothold in Mozambique, they built a station at the mouth of the River of Good Tokens – a station from which grew the port of Quelimane, as it is known today. The reason was a desire to penetrate to the "land of gold", the territory ruled over by chief Monomotapa. (If legend is to be believed, Monomotapa would have been well over 100 years old at this stage.) Attempts to reach the chief and his riches from Sofala, their only station south of the Zambesi River, had proved fruitless.

Monomotapa had a dignity equal to the early Portuguese discoverers and when word reached him that the White men with guns were looking for him, he took his golden secret and his wives in tow and started moving north. But the Portuguese quest for the legendary chief and his gold mines continued. Francisco Barreto, a former Viceroy of India, was instructed by King Sebastian to conquer the country for its gold, and in 1569 he set out with over 1 000 of his kinsmen to find Chief Monomotapa. It was cruel going even for the hardy Portuguese and they died in their droves from disease and the wild animals. Barreto was forced to abandon his quest.

Soon after his return to Sena, Barreto died, and legend says the elusive Monomotapa died on the same day at the spot where Nampula is situated today whence his dignified face rose from the earth in mocking defiance of his pursuers and as a lasting symbol of the old Africa before the White men came.

Fact or fable, the quest for Monomotapa's gold is a lovely story – part of the rich heritage of Mozambique.

It was in Nampula that we made our first contact with the Army. By chance we met a former army captain named Luis Correia at the Hotel Portugal in Avenida Antonio Enes. Correia is now the army's public relations officer and has a foot in every door of importance in the province. Through him we gained access to military headquarters, where we were briefed by the various sections on the Portuguese war effort one evening.

With us were two reporters from Cologne, in Germany, two of the many journalists we met in the territory and two of the less fortunate. They were particularly interested in the briefing as their visas were due to expire and this was their only chance of getting an overall picture before they had to fly out of Mozambique and return to Germany. It was also our only chance of presenting our programme to the army, so the briefing developed into a classical dog-eats-dog journalistic fracas in which the only thing that was resolved was that our German colleagues would have spent their time more profitably in their musty rooms back at the Hotel Portugal. It was a furious German party that flew out of Nampula the next day as we sat drinking coffee and discussing the programme we had foisted on the bewildered army officers the previous night. All we needed was the permission of the commander-in-chief of the armed forces, General Basto Machado.

We spent three days tying up the loose ends in Nampula, gathering information about the war and discussing it with Luis Correia, who proved to be a fount of information. "I want to write a book on the war one day," he told me. "Don't bother, Luis, I already have," I said. I don't think he believed me.

The Hotel Portugal intrigued us. It is the prestige hotel of Nampula, something that never ceased to amaze me as the entire period we were under its roof we were without water. Our afternoon siestas were interrupted regularly by the plumber – who turned out to be a page in the morning and waiter at night – with an assistant who believed that by turning on the sink tap he could exorcise the spirits that had rendered our shower impotent.

James Soullier, who was half asleep during the plumber's third intrusion, got up and walked to the bathroom.

"You've been here three times now and there's still no water." He borrowed the screwdriver from our Black persecutor, fiddled about for a few minutes, then poked his head round the door.

"Listen, this guy doesn't understand English; I don't speak Portuguese and he's driving me up the wall. His mate here has still got a fixation about the sink." He disappeared back into the bathroom and a monologue followed in a distinct Australian drawl. "Not the sink, fella; I don't bath in the sink – the shower! Here, look." I heard him clamber into the shower and fiddle about behind the plastic curtains.

"Shower. You see, wash? . . . no, not the sink. Look leave that alone. What do you think you can do with that screwdriver anyway? Spanner! . . . you need a spanner. God! I give up. Listen, mate, take your screwdriver and your Mickey Mouse friend here and leave us in peace – OK?" Jim emerged from the bathroom shaking his head. At that point the plumber seemed as fed up with us as we were with him – but he won the confrontation by urinating in the least important article of plumbing in our bathroom – the bidet, before walking out with a blend of Portuguese and African dignity.

This unlooked for entertainment probably accounted for the bill next morning – R50 for three nights, without the option of bed and breakfast. If you don't accept full pension at the Hotel Portugal, you can't get a room. This was a surprise to us because it was in conflict with the usual hospitality shown by most Portuguese. In fact, when we returned to Nampula, we moved into a pension and with a little persuasion got the landlady to cook breakfast for the two "senhors" at no extra cost.

Luis Correia is a large man with a shock of curly hair that tops off his bulky frame. He looked like the pictures of Brendan Behan during an all-nighter through the Dublin pubs. One afternoon we drove to Mozambique Island, stopping on the way to drive off into the bush. "I want to show you what the jungle is like in Cabo Delgado," said Luis, and without hesitating we veered off, parked the car and went crashing through the thick undergrowth on foot, fighting our way as the vines groped at our hands and feet with an almost challenging intent.

"People wonder why we keep so close together in the bush, now you can see for yourself. This area is exactly like the jungle in the north. Many of our troops have been killed by taking the easy way out – following the river beds and breaks in the jungle, instead of sticking to the bush. Sometimes we spend weeks under these conditions, living off the jungle. You get to understand it, even to like it. We have captured Frelimos who have been living off the jungle for nine years without ever returning to their bases in Tanzania. Many of the men we capture are emaciated, suffering from disease and malnutrition and semi-naked, which just shows you how dedicated, or at least misdirected some of them are."

As we cut our way slowly through the undergrowth, the jungle formed a steaming canopy above our heads so that only rarely did a pinprick of sunlight hesitantly creep through. I realised then just how exacting the fighting conditions in Mozambique are. When we finally got back to the car, we were bathed in sweat and eager to continue on our way to the island. What it must be like for combat troops, I shuddered to think.

Like Zanzibar, Mozambique Island is a cradle of romanticism and enchantment. It is the earliest vestige of European culture south of the Sahara and one of the few spots that has never been conquered by a second colonial power. This tiny gem in the Indian Ocean has withstood the elements and hostile powers ranging from the Dutch to the Moors for more than 450 years and the cultural interchange of Blacks, Arabs and Europeans and the religious mingling of Christian, Moslem and pagan has left the island community with an indefinable identity all of its own.

If the Portuguese were not at war, Mozambique Island would be my choice for an escape from the twentieth century with its commercialism and headlong rush for that ambiguous goal called "progress". But today the island has its part to play in a Portuguese war just as it has in others over the past four centuries.

The island is dominated by Fort de Sao Sebastiao, the Fort of Saint Sebastian, that juts out of the island like an angry thumb hitching a ride from the coral-studded ocean. The fort was built with the great quoins used in the Portuguese caravels as ballast on their voyages to India in the sixteenth century and it is the true symbol of Portugal in Africa.

Today the fort is out of bounds to tourists and visitors to the island and is used as a rest camp for operational troops before they go back into the bush in search of groups of Frelimo guerrillas.

With the necessary permissions of the mayor, a balding little man wearing a crumpled suit, and the army, we visited the fort, built by Vasco Gomes de Abreu to guard the sea route between Lisbon and India against the Arabs.

The day I visited this historic monument to early Portuguese chauvinism, the sixth company of Commandos, or the Sombres as they are better known in Mozambique, were billeted there, lapping up their fifteen-day holiday before being moved south to seek out and destroy Frelimo bands that were blowing up railway installations in the central province of Vila Pery that borders with Rhodesia.

The Sombres allegedly were responsible for the massacre of the entire population of Wiriyamu, near Tete. They are battle-hardened men, men who have stared death in the face on many occasions and men who have long lost their patience with journalists trying to get

27

at the truth behind Wiriyamu. In answer to my questions on the incident, a sergeant, who called himself Caesar, told me bluntly in impeccable English: "The Germans killed six-million Jews during the last war; do you think we could possibly labour under that type of stigma?" I didn't want to labour the point.

Inside the fort I was shown the armoury. In this tightly guarded building I was also shown captured Frelimo weapons. They were all either designed or manufactured in Russia, Red-China or Czechoslovakia: Kalashnikov AK47s, Simonov assault rifles, 60 and 80 mm mortars, bazookas, recoilless rockets and the latest Russian toy currently used by Frelimo in Cabo Delgado, the 122 mm missile. This weapon is launched from steel ramps inside Mozambique to attack the far flung army outposts along the Rovuma River, Mozambique's nothern border with Tanzania. I was to see the results of these missile attacks later in the shell-shocked garrison of Mueda, the "Da Nang" of Mozambique.

I found it sadly ironic that this armoury crammed with Communist weapons stood next to the earliest Christian church south of the equator, The Church of Our Lady of the Bulwarks. This lovely old church, with its Moorish design, whispers of the past. And a plaque embedded in its cobbled floor marks the grave of a Catholic Bishop of Japan, who was buried there in 1588.

Here were the weapons of war side by side with the oldest temple of God in Southern Africa, each with a message – one of love, the other of destruction.

Our return to Nampula that afternoon was a sad journey for me. The lingering memories of Mozambique Island kept returning: the timeless fishermen emptying their glittering harvest in the market place where the local shoppers haggle over prices as their forebears did centuries before them; the Governor's palace with its artistic treasures, elevated four-poster-beds lined with elaborate patterns of lace; the Church of Misericordia now converted to the island's post office and the densely populated African quarter where the women refuse to be photographed for religious reasons – all a pageant of time-worn beliefs and enchanting age.

As the twilight settled down and we ate a giant red-and-white-striped lobster at the Bagdad Restaurant in Nampula's Avenida Jose Cabral, I had my first introduction to one of the folk heroes of Mozambique, General of the Air Force Manuel Diogo Neto.

The evening's silence was shattered by the whine of a Fiat jet "buzzing" the sleepy town. "It's General Neto," said Luis, leaping up from the table and dashing outside. We followed and watched as the tiny fighter aircraft performed a perfect loop above the town before putting down its undercarriage and landing at the airport beyond as the sun made its gentle exit on another sweltering day.

"What's so special about that?" I asked. My meal had been interrupted and Mozambique lobsters are unequalled anywhere in the world except in Mauritius, and I wasn't particularly keen on forgetting the fact.

"He's just returned from a combat mission," said Luis. I thought it a bit odd that the chief of an air force should be flying combat missions.

"Tell me more," I said, and was told:

"General Neto runs the world's strangest operations centre – he conducts the air war from his flat in Nampula where he keeps in radio contact with his airmen throughout the territory.

"I took a journalist to meet him one night and we ended up finishing a bottle of whisky in his flat at two a.m.," said Luis. "General Neto decided that if he was up and about at that ungodly hour so too should be the air force chief in Tete. He radioed him from the flat, but he wasn't there. Ten minutes later a call came through from Tete; the officer had returned from a night on the tiles. The general exploded all over him and switched off the radio. But then he burst out laughing. He's really a mad guy."

After that story I wanted to meet the general. He is probably the only air force chief in the world who flies strike missions – and I was already planning an article along those lines.

"Where can I find him?" I asked.

Luis laughed. "In one of the pubs. He usually drinks with a corporal friend of his, the guy who services his jet."

Despite the general's buccaneer life-style, I heard mention of him throughout Mozambique in a different way – as one of Portugal's greatest airmen, a sound military tactician and one of Portugal's most highly decorated sons.

That night we scoured the pubs to find General Neto. Everywhere we went, he seemed to have beaten us to the mark. The next day we missed him again; he had left before dawn to bomb Frelimo camps in the north in his personal jet, known throughout the territory because of the scorpion insignia on the fuselage. And that night, I was told, he had left for Lisbon for an interview with Prime Minister Caetano. We had no way of knowing when he would return, but in the back of my mind I knew we would meet. My instincts proved correct, but of that later.

I wanted to meet this dashing airman, but I had also to learn something about the Portuguese Air Force in Mozambique.

I learned it was sadly lacking. It comprised 12 Fiat G91 fighter-bombers, seven DC3 (Dakotas), five Nord-Atlas transports, 15 converted Harvard T6 bombers, 14 Alouette helicopters, two Puma helicopters, an undetermined number of spotter planes and the DETA aircraft.

This information, on paper, suggested the strength of the Mozambique Air Force was highly questionable, to say the least, yet for 10 years Portuguese airmen have battled on bravely with their miserable collection of antiquated aircraft against an enemy that has sophisticated anti-aircraft weapons inside Mozambique and would soon back them up with the Russian-built SAM 7 or" Strella" ground-to-air missile,the same system that caused so much havoc in Vietnam and with the Israeli Air Force in the Yom Kippur War in 1973.

Life for the airmen is hazardous. Not only do they live in fear of anti-aircraft attacks from the dense jungle below, but they are often sniped at by Frelimo groups. While I was in Nampula, the commander of the military garrison on Mozambique Island, Lt.-Colonel Nuno Alvares Pereira, was shot dead in a Dakota flying near Mueda, in Cabo Delgado. It was a strange way to die. The aircraft was flying fairly low when a single bullet from a Chinese Kalashnikov automatic rifle ripped through the fuselage and passed through the elbow of a lieutenant sitting next to the colonel. The bullet then entered the colonel's side, passed through his body and re-entered his chin. He died immediately – the victim of an unseen enemy in the unseen jungle below. His killer may never have got to hear of his success.

We were sitting again at a boulevard table in Nampula, fast losing interest in the parade of people – just restless to get moving, to get away from the town and get on with the job. Nothing seemed to be happening and my constant reminders to our contact at Army headquarters had brought no results. We hadn't seen Luis for the past day and although everyone in Nampula knew him, nobody knew where he had gone.

We were waiting for him then, wondering if any progress had been made with our demands for permission to go north, to meet the soldiers, to get into the thick of the war and see what was really happening in the north.

The sun was like a hot lance, even through my sunglasses. Jimmy Soullier had left his at the hotel and I saw his eyes slowly close into slits to keep out the glare.

His fingers were drumming on the table. "We've been here three days already – when are we gonna get out of this Mickey Mouse outfit." Jim had not been impressed with Nampula and was itching to get something on film.

"A bit of patience, Jimmy – this is Africa not Sydney. Here's a thought – Camoes probably sat at this very spot 400 years ago."

"Who was Camoes?"

Strange how you can get a kick out of parading knowledge. "You mean you don't know about Camoes?" Here was the chance to slay an innocent audience of one. Little did Jimmy Soullier, late of Sydney Australia, know that I had brushed up on Portugal, Mozambique, Luis de Camoes, Vasco da Gama and Gil Vicenti, the Portuguese Shakespeare, for weeks before setting out on this assignment, but I wasn't about to tell him that.

"Camoes was one of Portugal's greatest poets and he lived 400 years ago," I said, warming to my subject. "He was quite a man and, like one of his ancestors, Vasco Perez de Cameos, he was a soldier-poet.

Jim had stopped drumming on the table.

"Sounds like quite a guy, but I bet he didn't have to hang around this dump for three days without having a shower," said Jim. The Hotel Portugal had really got to him.

"Camoes hung around Mozambique for three years trying to get back to Portugal on his return from India. One thing about that wait, though, even if like you he had left his sunglasses in his hotel it wouldn't have mattered – he only had one eye."

"How come?"

"He lost it fighting in the army in Africa and from then on went around with a patch over the damaged eye."

"Like that Jewish guy?"

"What Jewish guy?"

"General Duggan!"

"You make him sound like an Irishman – you mean Moshe Dayan?"

"Yeah. And like that Scandinavian guy, Nielsen; the one who died at Trafalgar – he also had a patch."

"Horatio *Nelson* . . ." But I didn't have to go on – the biter was being bitten, and Jimmy was grinning. The game was worth pursuing as there was nothing else to do at that stage except talk, drink coffee and wait. It was Jim's turn.

"Say, wouldn't it be a gag if Madame Tussaud's Waxworks in London slapped them all together – patches and all; each one with a card hung round his neck. I can see them now – General Dayan with a card which said 'I got my patch with the British Army'. And Camoes: 'I got my patch with the Portuguese Army'; and Nelson: 'But I got mine with the Royal Navy'."

"You've left one out."

"Who's that?"

"The biggest eye-patcher of them all – the man in the Hathaway Shirt." We both laughed.

Luis Correia nudged his bulky frame past a group of middle-aged Portuguese engrossed in a game of drafts – a great pastime in Mozambique – and walked over to join us.

"It's all right, everything's arranged, you leave for the north tomorrow," he said. Our game was over and we went back to the hotel, each with his own thoughts and me with the lasting image of a host of sightless soldiers in history's timeless march to war.

Before we left Luis outside the hotel entrance, I asked him where he had been.

"We went to photograph a Russian submarine a few kilometers off the coast of Mozambique Island. I can't tell you much about it yet, but I think it is beaming anti-Chinese propaganda through a powerful transmitter on board to Tanzania under the call sign of 'The Free Voice of Zambesi and Pemba'. We got the photographs before it even had a chance to submerge."

This confirmed what I already thought about Luis, he was more than a "public relations officer" and on many of the occasions that we discussed the war, I found him to be better informed than most of the army officers at military headquarters. Luis Correia indeed was an extraordinary man.

Top: A young Portuguese soldier being flown back to Lourenco Marques for hospitalisation. He was a victim of a mine blast in the north. This picture clearly shows how the DETA aircraft are sometimes used for military purposes.

Bottom: A group of regular troops and civilians are ushered onto a train on the Beira-Umtali railway line, which on average was being attacked once a week. On the left is one of a group of crack commandos, who with the militiamen, protect the trains.—Picture: James Soullier.

A THING OF THE PAST?
A Portuguese militiaman holds his FN rifle at the ready in case of attack on the
Beira-Umtali train by Frelimo guerrillas.—Picture: James Soullier.

CHAPTER THREE

THE ADMIRAL OF THE NAVY: PALMA

Captain Jorge Martino looked dejected. We had just put down at Porto Amelia airport, in Cabo Delgado, and been introduced to Colonel Voloso, commander of the army garrison at the port, and Captain Martino, who was to accompany us on our journey through the north.

"I have orders for you to go north," said Colonel Voloso. In Mozambique the "north" has the same type of connotation that the "Russian Front" had for the average German soldier during World War II.

"From Porto Amelia, you fly with the Admiral of the Navy to Palma and then on the Nangade and Mueda. Your plane leaves in 20 minutes," said the Colonel. "Or if you prefer, there is an armed convoy leaving Palma tomorrow for Pundanhar. If you go by convoy, a plane will fly you from Pundanhar to Nangade and Mueda whenever the convoy gets through."

There was no doubt in my mind we would opt for the convoy on the offchance of seeing some action. Palma, I knew, was a natural harbour near the mouth of the Rovuma River, Mozambique's northern border with Tanzania. The road the convoy would take follows the Rovuma for 50 km to Pundanhar. It then doubles back to a tiny military outpost called Nhica, five km from the Tanzanian border before branching back to Palma. The 100 km round trip, I also knew, was one of the most dangerous in Africa.

Jorge Martino looked awkward in his camouflage uniform. He was wearing sunglasses and in his right hand he held a cigarette holder. His dark Latin complexion was decidedly waxy as he joined in the conversation.

"It's much easier to fly direct to Nangade from Palma. The convoy to Pundanhar is dangerous and it sometimes takes over two weeks to travel that road by truck."

Colonel Voloso waited impatiently as James Soullier and I discussed it. We were already well into our second week in Mozambique and our visas were due to expire the following week. We certainly couldn't afford to spend two weeks travelling 50 km with a Portuguese army convoy. But, by this stage Jimmy was restless. Our tour thus far had given him little to photograph of value and one look at his face was enough to make up my mind.

"We'll take the convoy from Palma," I said. I glanced at Captain Martino; he was putting another cigarette in his holder. I couldn't see his face. Journalists in Mozambique are faced with one almost insurmountable problem. Because of the language barrier, army officers accompany you as interpreters on the war fronts. These officers are drawn from what the combat troops call "the air conditioning zone", and are usually very reluctant to enter the combat zones. I had heard stories from newsmen who had spent weeks wandering through the jungle on "patrols" in the hope of seeing action and returning with nothing because their officer companion had taken them on a wild goose chase to ensure his own safety.

Captain Jorge Martino was cast in a different mould. Jorge was a non-combatant based in Port Amelia. If any man had more right to protect his own skin, it was Jorge. His wife and family were back in Lisbon whence he had had to leave when he was drafted into the army for a second time. "I don't know how it happened," he told me one evening, "but here I am and there is nothing I can do about it."

We joined the naval party with their neatly starched white uniforms and left Porto Amelia behind as the six-seater air-taxi gained height and flew out over the ocean.

The jungle ended abruptly, giving way to one of the most alluring stretches of coast I have seen. Flying parallel to the shore, I could see the occasional Arab Dhow drifting listlessly among the coral islands that dotted the ocean beneath, their triangular sails heaving against the off-shore breeze. It reminded me of earlier days flying over the Greek Islands in the Mediterranian except these islands showed no sign of life or activity.

From the air, I could distinctly make out the contours of the ocean bed and even the occasional shoal of fish glittering beneath the surface like a twinkle in the ocean's turquoise eye.

The chief of the Navy, Admiral Moura da Fonseca, spoke to his aides in the seat ahead of us, occasionally pointing down at the ocean or making some remark to the pilot. Within a few minutes of take-off I had drafted a list of questions which I gave to Jorge to ask the admiral.

Admiral Moura da Fonseca took his time answering them. He was a short, balding man with neatly cut hair greying at the temples. As Jorge interrupted him with a deferential tap on the shoulder to put each question, the admiral seemed to glare at him with studied distaste, which is not unusual when naval officers deal with the army. Later I learnt it was the first time the admiral had been interviewed by the Press, and although the conditions were not appropriate for the occasion, he was savouring every moment.

Two things of interest emerged from this hurried interview. The admiral was clearly disturbed that an outsider, and a journalist to boot, should have known about the presence of a Russian submarine off Mozambique Island the previous day, but he did not attempt to avoid the question.

"As we know," he said, "the Soviet Navy is taking up positions against us. The presence of that submarine yesterday is not going to add anything to the actual situation."

His answer confirmed my information and only reinforced my admiration for Luis Correia's private intelligence network in Nampula.

The admiral also told me that the Cabora Bassa hydro-electric scheme, nearing completion on the Zambesi River, in Mozambique would increase the Navy's commitments in Mozambique. Once the project was completed, the dam would stretch back over 250 km of the Zambesi Valley towards the Zambian and Malawi borders. The navy was expecting to police those waters with motor patrol boats in an attempt to stop Frelimo infiltration from Zambia and Malawi into the central provinces of Mozambique.

We touched down at Palma airstrip an hour later. From the air above Palma, I caught my first glimpse of the Rovuma River, Mozambique's northern border with Tanzania, as it snaked through the thick jungle to the north of us.

To people approaching the Rovuma from the south, it has an almost mystical fascination. Flying near the river gives one a creeping sense of insecurity. On the other side of the Rovuma is "that place" – Tanzania; mysterious, dark and hostile. It is also the Rovuma that separates Portuguese troops from the Frelimo training camps in Tanzania. As such it is a symbol for the average Portuguese soldier, something like the Styx through whose Stygian waters death makes its silent progress. For it is across the Rovuma River that small bands of Frelimo come at night to lay their mines on the dirt tracks that link the Portuguese border posts, before retreating silently over the river again, under cover of darkness to the safety of their base camps.

In Cabo Delgado, most aircraft fly at maximum height except the Air Force helicopters that skim along at tree-top level. Once an aircraft is over a town or an army garrison, it spirals down in tight circles. Low flying is dangerous in Cabo Delgado and a number of commercial pilots bear testimony to narrow escapes they had had from Frelimo ground fire.

Like most of the airstrips serving the outposts in Cabo Delgado, Palma's was a narrow strip of grass. On either side were Portuguese soldiers with their rifles at the ready, presumably in case of an attack.

It was the first place we had been in Mozambique where we were out of the hands of the civilian authorities. Throughout Mozambique the Portuguese secret police, DGS, held strict control of everybody's movements. At every departure point we were required to fill out forms relating our movements for the DGS. This was a requirement regardless of whether we were flying a mere 50 km. Each airport is classified as an international airport, which not only raises the landing fees (at Tete they were R22 for a private aircraft, R5 more than at Johannesburg's Jan Smuts Airport), but also requires that the traveller fills out immigration forms. Immigration was run by DGS. Every hotel in Mozambique required by law the filling in of two forms – one for the hotel records and one for DGS. The latter had to be delivered to the local DGS official within 24 hours. It was also common practice to have our passports removed for DGS scrutiny. They were always returned later the same day.

These formalities may seem quaint to the average tourist, but the longer we stayed in Mozambique, the more irksome they became and the more aware we became of the omnipresence of DGS.

Palma was quite different. It is a military post and also houses one of Mozambique's largest and best developed "aldeamentos", or fortified villages.

These aldeamentos have been built throughout the north and more recently in the central provinces to "control" and "protect" the local population.

Portuguese policy has been to attract the local villagers out of the jungle to the aldeamentos where educational and medical facilities are provided by either the civilian or military authorities. In many of the aldeamentos the military and the civil arm work together. The aldeamentos are one of Portugal's most controversial policies in her African territories. In Mozambique, they have been called the "human Maginot Line" and are the key to Portuguese efforts to reduce Frelimo subversion and to drag the indigenous population into the strange ways of a modern cash economy.

The Frelimo propaganda agency, which is highly developed inside Mozambique and in the international arena, has branded the aldeamentos as "concentration camps". When you visit them it is obvious that this is a false claim. The aldeamentos range in size from 200 to 3 000 people depending on soil conditions, water supply and tribal structures.

The Mozambique I saw already had 900 established aldeamentos, housing a million people, many of them protected by local militiamen. In the little open-sided schoolhouses the children sing the Portuguese national anthem for visitors and their rousing little voices followed me in most of the aldeamentos I visited.

That is part of the mystery of Mozambique – that a class of near-illiterate Black children can sing the praises of Portugal with a swell of pride and an innocent beauty that only the African voice can produce, while all around them more intelligent minds plot new methods of reinforcing or destroying their innocent allegiance to Mother Portugal.

Life in Palma is as one would expect to find on some isolated island in the Pacific. Everything grows in profusion in Palma and the great coconut palms reach up to the sky like lonely supplicants to a god unseen.

The "administrative" section of Palma, which in colonial days would have been the "European" sector, looks down from a small plateau on to the palm-fringed lagoon below.

As you drive down to the lagoon, you are transported as if by magic into the old Africa: circular huts made of mud and straw; elegantly patterned square houses with bamboo fences; naked children with strings of pastel-shaded coral-fish swinging at their sides; bantams fluttering across the cinder streets, and young women, their naked breasts heaving with sensuality beneath the great rice baskets or loads of firewood carried on their heads with great skill.

37

Palma aldeamento is a mixture of tribes and religions: Catholic, Protestant, Moslem, Macua, Ajana, Angoni and Maconde. It was my first contact with the Macondes – one of Africa's great tribes and one of the continent's few people who have constantly resisted any form of outside domination.

They are a proud race of people and undoubtedly rank with South Africa's Zulus as one of Africa's greatest warrior tribes.

The women have a distinct beauty that sets them apart from most of the African peoples. They carry it with a rare primitive grace despite the deep tribal scars that are cut into their cheeks and foreheads during their initiation ceremonies. Some, the older ones, still have discs in their lips and plugs through their noses. Their teeth are filed into sharp points when they are young as, traditionally, they are meat-eaters and it gives them that bit of added glamour for their menfolk. The filing of their teeth is an extremely painful process and today has largely been discontinued.

The men have an overbearing air of aloofness that shines out of them with arrogant condescension.

The Macondes, 100 000 of whom are inside Mozambique, have been a constant headache to the Portuguese, who consider them 90 per cent subverted by Frelimo. Those who have accepted Portuguese authority have been slow to adapt. Warriors by nature, the placid agricultural life and alien diet of fish and rice in Palma, are as repulsive to the average Maconde as a bone plug through the nose would be to the average Portuguese.

"I don't understand them," said a Portuguese colleague in Palma. "There is more food in the ocean than they could wish to eat, but they refuse to fish." To the maritime Portuguese this may appear sinful; to the Macondes it is "the work of children and sick men," they say.

Many of the women wear a type of beauty mask and you can often see them with their faces hidden behind a white mask of congealed sap from a tree that grows throughout the north. Once a day they clean their teeth with a black root, but when I tried it it burnt my tongue and left my lips glowing with a red stain like a new Elizabeth Arden lipstick.

As we drove through the aldeamento, the residents dropped whatever they were doing, or stood to attention beside the road and doffed their hats. Those who were without headgear saluted as we drove past, but I noticed no sign of recognition from the women, who stood in silence.

The governor, a great jovial character with a red face and enormous smile, raised his right hand in a regal gesture as we swept past in our state-owned Land-Rover. It reminded me of the British Raj as I had always pictured it, and echoed some past era when the White man was a deity in the Third World.

The governor seemed a total anachronism in modern-day Africa. Yet there he was like a British administrator raising his right hand to the deferential crowds before Nkrumah's rhetoric began to topple the White idols. It occurred to me that this man was the living personification of all that emergent Africa despises. And yet a warmer man I have yet to meet.

Down at the waterfront again we saw the admiral, his diminutive figure walking delicately across the sand to where it merged into the lagoon. Although he had an audience, he remained unembarrassed, gently aloof as he rolled up his starched trousers, glanced over his shoulder and waded out to a rowboat bobbing 10 metres from the shore. I had expected his aides to chairlift him through the water, but he waved them away and Jimmy Soullier caught him on film for posterity – hands on his hips beside his rowboat with his aides fussing around him like pilot fish. That is how I will always remember Admiral Moura da Fonseca, his usually harassed face a picture of calm as the warm waters of the Indian Ocean splashed playfully about his knees.

The governor's house was like a dream. We sat on the lawn outside as the last touch of sunlight painted a farewell to the day across the lagoon below. Our thoughts were far away. It was a moment of magic drawn from the pages of life that will leave its image on my mind for future recall in moments of loneliness and nostalgia.

It was there that all the rich history of Portugal came vividly to life from the misty recess of mind, as early evening noises sang a plaintive fado; it was more – it was Amalia Rodriques, Portugal's greatest singer with her lovely voice seducing the inhabitants of the lagoon and holding off the night a few moments longer.

The Governor's wife was a Mullato, an elegant women adorned with fine jewellery that reminded me of the intricate silverwork made on Ibo Island off the coast of Mozambique, near Porto Amelia.

It was a strange evening. Our interpreter, Jorge Martino, unwittingly had forgotten a point of social etiquette and to this day I don't know the name of the Governor or his fine lady. Instead of talking, we nodded our approval of the lady's table – something that pleased her immensely – and we smiled thankfully each time the Governor filled our glasses with golden Bucelas wine, one of Portugal's treasures.

It was Bucelas wine that is reputed to have saved the life of George III of England. It is a nice story. George III was suffering from an incurable disease before he came to the throne. Then he was introduced to Bucelas wine by the Duke of Wellington who had brought it back as a gift from his campaigns in Portugal. The wine is said to have cured him and the king is reputed to have stayed loyal to it for the rest of his life. The dry wine, with its slightly acid bite, was the perfect antidote to the lady's fiery peri-peri sauce that brought the sweat to my face and a knowing smile to the Governor's lips.

It saddened me to hear later in my journey through Mozambique that the Governor was to be transferred and would have to leave his little paradise behind. His house, which he aptly called "Palace a Grande", I thought would seem very empty without this couple with their grace and affection. To me, the Governor of Palma will always remain a symbol of the Portuguese character at its very best.

Early the next morning, Captain Carlos Moas collected us from the "Palace a Grande" and drove us to the army shooting range, a few kilometres from Palma.

He handed me a G3 automatic – the Portuguese standard weapon – and five magazines of live ammunition, then stood back as I slipped the first magazine into the rifle, cocked it and released the safety catch.

This weapon, the G3 automatic rifle, in my opinion, is superior to the South African R1. It is fully automatic and is a durable weapon which stands up to tough treatment in war conditions. I have handled both and prefer the G3.

I've also handled the Kalashnikov AK47, the Chinese-made Russian-designed fully automatic rifle which many Frelimo use, and I consider this one to be the best of the lot, even though the one I used was made just after World War II.

The bullets thudded dully into the pit at the head of the shooting range. By the time I had emptied four magazines, shooting from different positions and from the hip, Captain Moas seemed satisfied I could handle the weapon.

"Your turn," he said turning on Jimmy Soullier.

"No thanks. The only shooting I will be doing will be with my camera," said Jimmy. Little did he know.

Back at the army camp we drew our camouflage outfits and little peaked caps, combat rations and ammunition. It took all my persuasive powers to convince Captain Moas that I didn't want any of the five hand-grenades he tried to foist on me. Instead, he swopped my G3 automatic for his own personal weapon. "It's more lucky," he said.

It was 8 a.m. The trucks were loaded and ready to roll out of Palma. As we walked over to take our place on the 6th truck, Captain Moas gave us our last-minute instructions.

"If any of the trucks are mined, don't jump out of the truck, Frelimo often lays anti-personnel mines as well. If you are ambushed, lie flat in the back of the truck and only start shooting when the troops open fire. It is for your own safety.

"Boa Sorte" he said, then shaking my hand walked back to his office briskly. Nobody on the war front of Mozambique ever says goodbye, only "boa sorte" – good luck.

CHAPTER FOUR

CONVOY IN THE NORTH: PUNDANHAR

The convoy followed the deeply rutted track as it left Palma behind, its memories fading with each new bend in the road. Behind was the Mozambique I would like to remember, tranquil and relaxed, ahead a hostile territory under the same flag, but without the niceties of Portuguese culture. Ahead lay Cabo Delgado outside the fence of military protection, the mystical "north" where so many soldiers and civilians, many innocent villagers, have died ignobly beneath the scorching equatorial sun.

Commanding the convoy was a young Portuguese officer, Lieut. Antonio Marques Pereira. He was slightly built with the wiry body of a long-distance runner. His dark hair protruded beneath his camouflage cap emphasising strong features. He looked more like a young Spanish student in his black T-shirt than a Portuguese officer and, like most of the young front line officers from metropolitan Portugal, he had a cavalier attitude toward his men and his mission.

Antonio was in his early twenties and was a graduate from Qoimbra University in Portugal. Most of the officers in the Mozambique army are graduates. It seemed strange that this young man, nurtured through an education in a country where nearly 70 per cent of the population is illiterate, should end up in the front line in Mozambique. Many of the young men faced with two and a half years of conscription and the prospect of fighting in one of Portugal's African territories leave Portugal. At the time of writing, 10 000 young men were leaving Portugal each year. Most of them emigrate to make new lives for themselves, but many end up like so many American conscientious objectors – frustrated expatriates inwardly wishing they could return to their mother country.

Since the military coup d'etat in Portugal and the heady freedom that followed, many of these men have returned to Portugal to savour Portugal's new-found freedom after nearly 50 years of dictatorship.

I was interested to see the reaction of Lieutenant Pereira and his men to our little trio. We must have seemed right out of place;

Jimmy Soullier, a diminutive Australian with red hair; Jorge Martino, a soft-spoken and gentle 6ft. administrative captain slightly overweight puffing away at his cigarette holder and myself, 6 ft. 3 in. softened through a sedentary life in cities from New York to London to Johannesburg. To make it worse, where the regular soldiers in Mozambique try every dodge imaginable to avoid the dangerous convoy duty in the north, there we were volunteering. We immediately got tagged as "the mad guys" by Lieutenant Pereira and his dishevelled band of bush veterans.

The track was more like a permanent scar on the bush than a road. Great parallel ruts ran along its path where the heavy vehicles' wheels had dug deep into the earth. In some places we had to stop and build the road up with earth, rocks and branches in case the trucks caught their radiators on the centre of the road which protruded from the dust track like a wall. In other places the floods had washed the track away, leaving a pile of broken trees and washed-up sand in their wake.

It was tortuous going. The vehicles were spaced 20 to 30 metres apart, but even at that distance we often had to stop and wait a few moments to catch sight of the truck directly behind as the road twisted its way through the thick bush.

Interspersed among the military vehicles, all French-designed Berliets built in Portugal, were the civilian trucks, which on occasions had to be dragged out of the deep ruts in the track. The four-wheel drive Berliet is ideal for those conditions. The Portuguese army in Mozambique formerly used Unimog troop carriers as escorts on these convoys, but when land mines became more pronounced, they were outlawed as they could not absorb the concussion of a mine explosion and too many men were getting killed.

The Portuguese use the Berliets as guinea-pigs. The first two trucks of the convoy were Berliets loaded with sand and driven by volunteer drivers. They drove slightly ahead of the main body of the convoy to explode any mines in the track. The others followed in their fresh tracks because to deviate, even by a few centimetres, could mean death to the driver and passengers of a following truck. The truck's wheels are filled three-quarters full with water, a trick the Portuguese learnt from the South Africans, so that if a wheel struck a mine, part of the concussion would be absorbed before it hit the truck's belly.

The jungle on either side of the track was scattered and patchy. In some places it formed a steaming canopy over our heads, malevolant and hostile, then it would break into open grassland before plunging back into thick, impenetrable bush. The Portuguese call it "jungle". In fact, it is very akin to the type of bush one finds in areas like the Kruger National Park, the famous game reserve in the north east of South Africa, except that in Cabo Delgado it is thicker, often restricting your vision up to three or four metres.

We had travelled about 25 kilometres when a dull explosion ripped through the air directly ahead of us. Our truck came to a sharp halt and we lay tense in the bottom of the truck as a wisp of cordite drifted past in the heavy air. The tenseness was almost tangible and except for the distinctive clicks of the safety catches on our rifles, there was complete silence; even the cicadas had stopped singing as we waited for something, anything to happen.

The truck directly in front had lurched on to its side, its left front tyre splayed across the track like a ruptured balloon. The silence was broken by Lieutenant Pereira, who on hearing the explosion, had jumped off his truck regardless of the danger and run back to the spot. He fired a burst into the surrounding bush before the troops jumped clear of the convoy and positioned themselves on either side of the road in case of an ambush.

"Stay in the truck", shouted the young lieutenant, "there may be more mines". Then, turning on his heel, he moved off into the bush to take command of the troops who were nervously watching the undergrowth for any sign of enemy movement.

There is a set procedure in these situations. Our truck, being next in line, drove backwards and forwards in the track behind the crippled vehicle to explode any other mines that might have been laid in or near the stretch of road. This is to ensure the safety of the men who have to repair the damage. That done, the mechanics got to work, propped up the mined vehicle and began changing its tyre.

Lieutenant Pereira reappeared walking down the side of the convoy giving orders to his men. In one hand he carried his G3 automatic, under the other arm, a case of beers. As he passed the mined vehicle, one of the mechanics handed him something, then he came over to join us in the back of our truck.

"Here", he said, "take these". He handed the beers up to me then clambered into the truck. "Anti-personnel", he said and handed me a

44

fragment of the mine recovered by the mechanic. "It doesn't do much to a Berliet, but it will take your legs off". He didn't labour the point, I had seen the results of those mines in the military hospitals. I noticed it was a fragment from a Portuguese plastic mine, part of the circular ribbed cap of the standard anti-personnel mine the Portuguese use in Mozambique. It had obviously been retrieved by a Frelimo group from the periphery of one of the army base camps which are sometimes surrounded by limited mine fields.

The standard Frelimo mine is made of wood or plastic, mostly made in China. These weapons are particularly dangerous as the only metal component in them is the detonator and a mine-detector cannot pick up its presence underground. Frelimo also uses a mine called the "jumping Jenny", an anti-personnel mine that springs up into the air when trodden on exploding at shoulder height. It is somewhat like a mine the South African forces met with so frequently in the Western Desert in World War II. It can tear a man in half, but is a small threat to a sturdy vehicle.

Another mine that has proved troublesome to the Portuguese is the ratchet mine which can be set to explode after any number of trucks have passed over it making all vehicles whether at the front or back of a convoy vulnerable.

I was surprised to see how nonchalant Lieutenant Pereira was considering a few moments before a truck had been crippled and we stood the chance of being attacked by mortars or even small arms fire from the bush. He had opened the case of Laurentina and was handing the warm beer around. The initial shock of the explosion was still ringing in my ears, but he seemed to have forgotten it had occurred.

"How often does this happen?" I asked.

"You see that man," he said pointing to the driver of our truck. "He has been blown up four times already on this road. There are always mines on this road." I looked at his face carefully. I could see from his eyes it was no exaggeration. I heard later that 35 mines had been recovered in a ten-kilometer stretch of the road a month previously.

I was surprised to hear this as the Portuguese employ a tactic against mines in their African wars that has been highly successful. Before a convoy leaves a base, a group of highly trained men leave ahead of the trucks on foot to sweep the road clear of mines. The picadores, as they are aptly called, push long bamboo poles with steel prongs on the end in the wheel tracks along the road.

These picadores are like the pikemen of the bullring only without their horses. They seem to have invested themselves with the courage and bravado of the bullring as they wield the "garrocha" (pike) in front of them, while each evil mine is a metal bull, a wicked bull, silently challenging and threatening anyone in its path. Frelimo mines are usually laid in haste under cover of darkness only inches beneath the road's surface. The sharp prongs of the picadores' poles upend the mines as they probe expertly beneath the surface and although they are supposed to bring enemy mines back to base, they usually explode them on the spot.

Each base along the border has its own group of picadores and there is a fierce rivalry between groups. These men, usually led by a white officer or sergeant, are as hardy as they are brave. Not only do they stand the chance of being ambushed as they probe the roads for mines or even of treading on one, but they have to walk up to 50 kilometres a day in full kit in heat that saps your energy and leaves you physically and mentally lethargic.

The picadores bear a heavy responsibility for to miss a mine in the road means possible death to the passengers of a truck following them. It is a responsibility they take on themselves with a certain panache, regarding themselves as elite troops and the backbone of Portuguese supply systems in the north. Strangely enough, very few of them are ever injured.

Among the picadore groups I spent time with, both in the north and the central provinces, only four fatalities had been recorded in the past year and one of them had died from a snake bite. The snake, I was told, had pierced the soldier's leather boot as if it were a piece of cardboard. He had shrugged the bite off as they were unable to identify the viper and continued on his way. He dropped dead in his tracks two kilometres further up the road. He knew the group wasn't carrying anti-snake serum and had decided to walk to his death like a man – a manifestation of that enigmatic quality displayed by so many Portuguese which we glibly call fatalism. Perhaps there is a better word for it in the Portuguese vocabulary. That better word would be "pundonor", dignity.

"But what about the picadores?" I asked the lieutenant. "Do they often miss mines in the road?"

"It is impossible to detect all the mines, the picadores are only human. Four trucks passed that mine and the fifth one exploded it. The driver didn't keep to the tracks. He was as much to blame." Twenty minutes later the case of beer was finished, the mechanics had fixed the mined Berliet and we were inching our way through the bush again.

We had travelled a further five kilometres when a shattering explosion erupted above the steady drone of the trucks. A cloud of smoke and fine dust filtered up into the air ahead and the distinctive crackle of automatic fire echoed back down the track.

"What the hell's going on up there?" I shouted to Jorge Martino, who was ducking low in the front of the truck with three Black troops.

"Could be an ambush. I don't know," he shouted back. And then the silence settled down again. But it was a silence that was making a noise in the uncertainty it brought with it. We could just see the tailboard of the truck ahead, nothing else. Those few moments were an agony of waiting indecision. In those few seconds after the vastly stronger explosion, my mind conjured up images of broken bodies and shattered victims further up the rutted track. Nobody spoke or moved – we simply lay there waiting and letting our anxious minds take flight.

The cicadas were back – a full orchestra of sound. The explosion had silenced them as though a martinet of a conductor had rapped his music stand and threatened them all with extinction if they didn't keep quiet. First there were a few timid scrapes from a nervous violin, followed by an errant plucking of strings, and then the whole orchestra burst into a wave of noise which indicated that life was back to normal – "you can all relax; the danger's over." Up ahead we could hear movement and the occasional stacatto burst of small arms fire as it ripped into the bush. The two-way radio in the truck behind us crackled into life. The static-laden voice told us the front truck had hit an anti-tank mine. Lieutenant Pereira was already at the head of the convoy and we heard his voice take over the radio and call on the convoy behind to tighten up its formation.

"Also bring those three mad guys up here," he said. "But not on foot, bring their truck up through the bush, then get the vehicles behind to close up ranks".

Our truck veered off the road and went crashing through the bush, knocking down trees in its path as we inched closer to the head of the convoy. The lead Berliet lay on its side, its left fender buckled upward from the concussion of the explosion. It lay in a pool of diesel oil and water where it had exploded the mine. The truck's front wheel had been blown 20 metres off into the bush, a formless mass of twisted metal and scorched rubber.

As we approached the shattered vehicle, I saw the driver, a young man with a delicate almost effeminate face, sitting by the side of the road, his head in his hands. The front of his camouflage smock had been ripped apart as his body was flung against the steering wheel, now bent into an obscene caricature of its former shape. His chest had been cut by the impact of his body smashing up against the steering wheel and already the skin was beginning to bruise about the small gold crucifix that had been pushed right into his torn flesh like a golden tattoo. The index finger of his right hand was dislocated and pointed at his right ear, and his whole body was heaving from the shock of the explosion.

A soldier walked up to him and roughly yanked the broken finger back into place, tapped him on the back of the head then walked off into the bush to join the other troops. It was a totally impersonal act, nothing Samaritan about it, simply righting a wrong. The camaraderie manifests itself in the bars and cafes of the cities. In the bush the men's more basic natures take over, self-preservation and the emotionless helping hand to a colleague in trouble.

We left the truck apprehensively. I could feel myself making a conscious effort to tread lightly, to try and feel the tell-tale hump in the ground where a mine may have been silently awaiting my boot. The troops had positioned themselves in a wide arc around the convoy in case of attack. It was here that I met the casual bomber. One of the soldiers was lobbing 60 mm mortars into the surrounding bush. It was amazing to watch. He would have given a mortar instructor back at his base an apoplectic fit to see how he was breaking all the rules by turning himself into a one-man artillery regiment with his rapid mortar fire. He had developed his own style with a mortar. He slipped it under his left armpit and wrenched the pin out of each bomb with his teeth in a steady, smooth action, slipping the projectiles into the mortar tube with his right hand. I counted carefully the number of bombs he put in the air

48

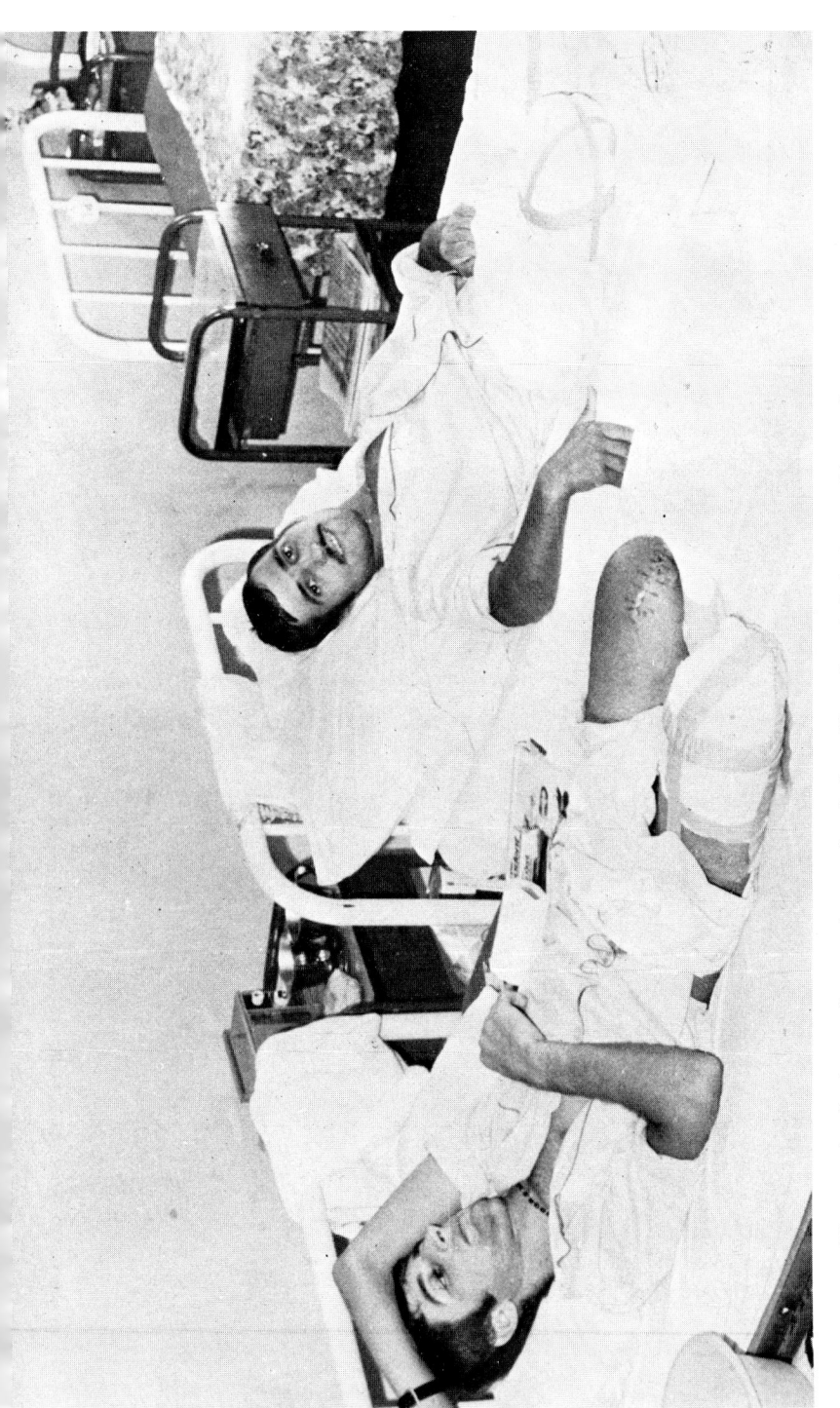

The tragedy of mine warfare can be seen in all the military hospitals in Mozambique. These two men were re-covering in Lourenco Marques.—Picture: Courtesy *Rand Daily Mail*.

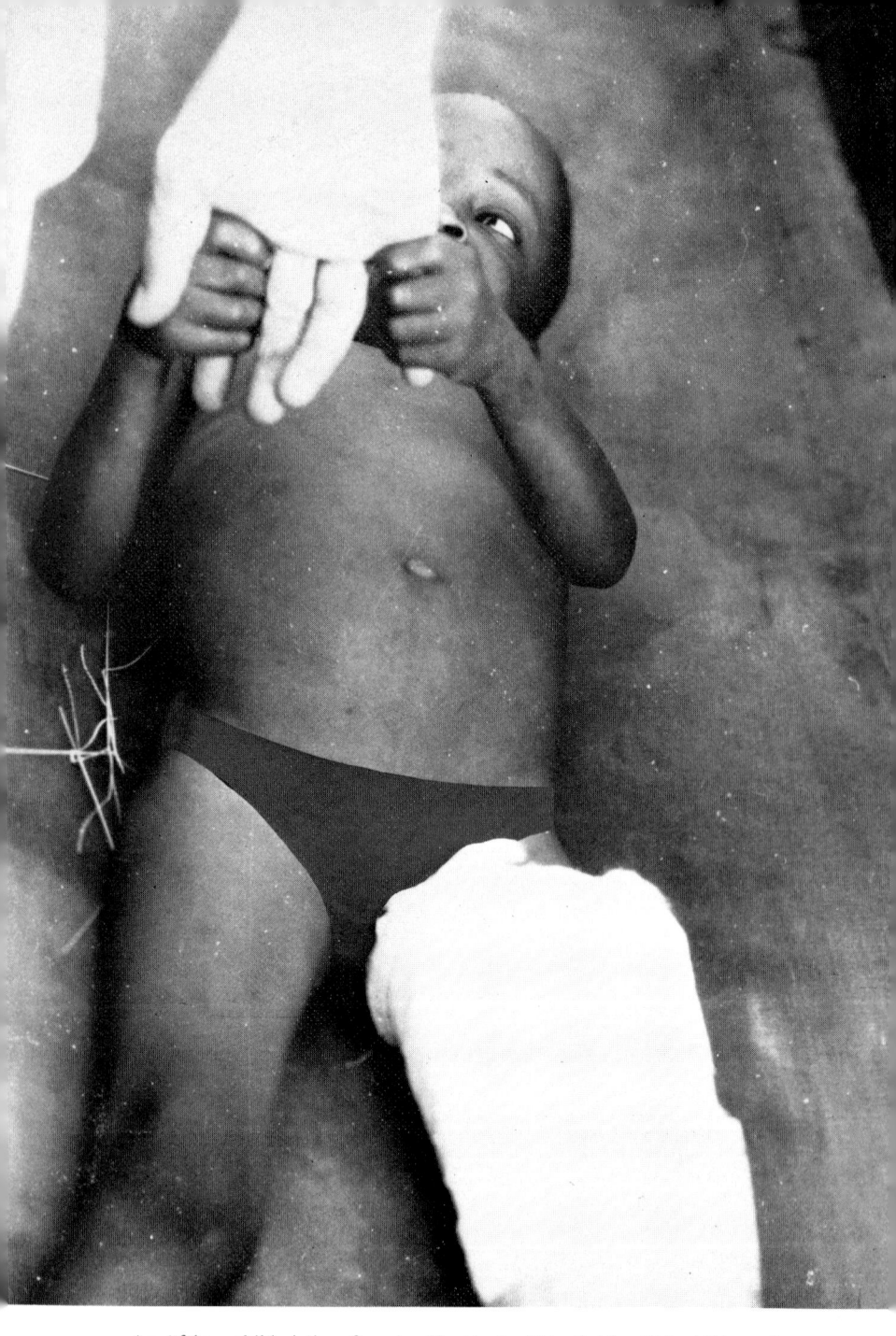

An African child victim of a mine blast in the Tete district. This child was fortunate, it only lost one leg. In most cases when a child treads on a mine, it loses both limbs.

before the first one exploded in the distant bush. By the time the first one exploded, he had put 10 bombs in the air, changing the angle and degree of the tube slightly with each one.

Nobody took any notice, but I had never seen anything like it before, one slight slip or misjudgment would have cost that man his life as a mortar is a lethal weapon to handle and at the time I thought it was suicidal to use that unconventional method. However, it was not long after that he persuaded me to try it myself and although it was a novel experience, I inwardly prayed for a return to convention.

After the initial excitement was over, Lieutenant Pereira rejoined us with another case of beer. We sat and talked about the war on the side of the road while the mechanics got to work and the troops maintained their silent watch in the bush beyond.

"We don't want to fight this war. You must understand we are all conscripts on these convoys, none of us are professional soldiers. I am only here as punishment," said a thickset sergeant who came to join us.

"I am only here because of an argument I had with a chico in Porto Amelia. Those chicos are bastards. You know about all the stuff that is sent to us from people in South Africa. Last Christmas a lot of food parcels were sent to the troops from friends in South Africa. Well, we never saw any of them – not one reached us here because the chicos keep them. They sell the contents on the black market in places like Nampula."

It was not the first time I had heard the fighting men accuse the professional soldiers, whom they call chicos, of black marketeering. A contact of mine in Nampula told me a shipment of air-conditioners had been sent to the military hospital in Nampula only to find their way into the officers' quarters while the injured were left to swelter in the heat of Nampula Hospital's depressing surroundings.

During World War II hundreds of South African women formed themselves into committees under the patronage of Mrs (Ouma) Smuts, wife of Field Marshal Smuts. They were a dedicated distaff army who packed linen bags with razor blades, sweets, socks, penknives and other useful items.

The bags were most welcome to the South African servicemen, who christened them Ouma's Glory Bags, but these, too, led to bad feeling and the belief that the bags were systematically rifled by un-

49

scrupulous servicemen who had access to them before delivery at the front.

Among the conscripts there seemed to be a general distaste for the professional army. I was to find this discontent simmering close to the surface everywhere we went in the territory. The swarthy sergeant continued: "We could finish this war and go home to our families, but the chicos don't want to finish the war, they're making too much money out of it. And there is nothing we can do because sometimes it is better to keep quiet and not make trouble. But you can tell people about what is happening to the things being sent to us, they can't do anything to you.

"You can go and see for yourself in the officers' mess in Nampula. South African cigarettes and chocolate, it's all there, but we never see any of it." I did not get an opportunity to check this sergeant's claims, but the indictment of the professional army was echoed by many people, some of them outsiders who appeared to have no axe to grind.

It took us hours to drag the crippled Berliet out of its watery grave and hitch it up to another vehicle to be towed to Pundanhar. The Portuguese never leave mined vehicles behind. They remove all physical evidence of damaged trucks as they believe it is bad propaganda to leave evidence of Frelimo successes. But there is no way of disguising the great gaping craters along the road. Rather than fill them in, the road makes a detour around each new crater. Some of these craters are large enough to swallow a small car.

The troops with us recalled each explosion as we passed the craters and vividly described each incident. These craters are like milestones on a sad journey to destruction. Only two weeks before, four men had been killed and three injured on this road when their vehicle exploded a makeshift mine. It was discovered later that the mine had been attached to a Portuguese bomb that had failed to explode during a bombing raid of a Frelimo base camp inside Mozambique. Apparently this was common practice in Cabo Delgado as similar incidents were related to me in other places.

In Mueda, the shell-shocked capital of the north, I was shown a number of vehicles badly damaged by these makeshift mines. Among them was the Berliet in which the four soldiers had been killed. The entire rear section of the truck had been torn from the chassis and curved upwards, fingers of twisted metal stretching toward the sky.

I found it surprising only four men had died in the explosion. By the time we had attached the mined truck to another Berliet it was late afternoon. We had spent five hours sitting at that spot in the middle of nowhere and we had to decide whether to stay in the jungle overnight or to push on to Pundanhar garrison, which by this stage I was beginning to think was a figment of the Portuguese imagination.

Lieutenant Pereira radioed ahead to report on our progress. "Those guys at Pundanhar say we must continue." He was smiling. "They say they have plenty of cold beer and warm brandy for us. If we don't come they say they'll drink it all." That was enough incentive to push on. The young officer had shown a remarkable capacity along the way. "If you don't drink on these convoys, you go out of your head, very mad," was his way of justifying it. None of us argued, and the beer flowed freely for the remainder of the trip.

The troops piled back into the trucks and once again we were on our way. The bush began to open up, giving a clear view for 50 metres on either side of the road. We drove hurriedly into the gathering sunset, apprehensive still, but warm in the knowledge that every kilometre was bringing us closer to safety.

The sun dipped below the trees lighting their heavy foliage with bright ambers and full-blooded reds which seemed to hang on the dust from our vehicles reflecting a secure warmth as we clung to the sides of the vehicle. With the sun down, the lead trucks speeded up like thirsty horses with the smell of water in their flared nostrils galloping back to the stable, uncontrolled, majestically unconcerned for the safety of the riders.

The headlights pierced the gathering gloom, illuminating the baobab trees as we sped past. They looked to me like surrealistic gendarmes, their fat bellies protruded and outstretched arms waving us on for I felt an almost tangible need for haste to leave the memories of that day behind.

The truck had become our castle. It represented a temporary home, a retreat from the hostility of an outside world we could neither understand nor control. It was as if we were flying up and away from the past only to level off on some new plain where at least we could comprehend our more basic emotions and desires. A cold beer had become a symbol of safety, something that neither seemed strange nor ridiculous in the circumstances.

We only made one more brief stop en route when a small, bewildered buck got caught in the headlights, its great eyes transfixed with the glare. The truck in front slowed down, and there was the sharp, cruel noise of a rifle above the engines and the animal dropped on to its forelegs, looked up at us in what seemed to be a puzzled manner as though saying as it plaintively bowed its gentle head in death: "Why me? What did I do wrong?"

The carcass was lifted into the back of the truck where it lay in a small pool of blood, a mute reminder of man's instinct to kill. Perhaps there was a salutory lesson in this incident, that the transition from killing an animal to killing a man is not difficult to make, that sublimated and hovering close to the surface in every man is, if not the desire to kill, at least the ability to do so. I was to find that when a man is confronted with the prospect of death each day of his life, the value of life is minimised and that much of the bravado of men in combat situations is really little more than a total acceptance of their own death, if not physical then spiritual.

It was not uncommon to find, with a little gentle questioning, that lurking beneath the hardened facades of many Portuguese soldiers was a quivering emotional animal totally lost with the mental scars that their exposure to the war had etched on their minds. Scratch beneath the surface of many of the men and you will find confusion and self-recrimination that lingers long after the presence of death has taken flight.

For the remaining two hours of the journey we were thrown about in the back of the trucks. All thought of caution seemed to have dissipated with the enveloping darkness and the calls of the bush were lost in the endless whine of the engines.

Those were strange moments. It was as if darkness, for once, was the protector, maternal and comforting. Night was our guardian and the dangers around us had been swallowed up in her protective cloak.

It was a weary party that eventually limped into Pundanhar garrison, with little to announce us but the grinding of gears and the audible sighs of relief from the troops sharing our truck. I watched Lieutenant Pereira standing on the top of his vehicle counting us in like a mother hen with her chickens. He waved the last truck in then sat down heavily as the convoy rolled into the camp along the side of its airstrip. The windsock hung limply on its wooden flagpole.

The entire military and civilian population of Pundanhar had turned out to greet our arrival; the soldiers in T-shirts or ragged camouflage uniforms and the civilians in their odd mixture of Western and traditional dress. There was great excitement among the civilians who danced about the trucks as if a liberation army had just released them from the yoke of some imaginary oppressor.

The little military outpost was like a converted tribal village. The road ran right through the centre of the camp: on one side some hastily erected military buildings, all jerry built as if for planned obsolescence. On the other side of the road were the African civilian houses reminiscent of any tribal village in Africa except for a small area where an underground shelter had been built for the soldiers in case the base was attacked. Behind the general administrative building, which housed the radio and the commanding officer's quarters were bomb shelters for mortar attacks and a number of the buildings were partially protected with sand bags.

Introductions were brief; traditional Portuguese formalities had long gone by the board with these men, some of whom had lived in that lonely outpost for 18 months or more. The captain commanding Pundanhar showed us to his room with little ceremony and was adamant we take over his quarters for the duration of our visit. The captain had a very dark complexion, his mouth ringed with dark stubble as if a graphic artist had worked on him with a lead pencil. A tatty old T-shirt barely covered his expansive stomach which he made no pretence in trying to hide. He was one of those men who says everything with his eyes – totally undemonstrative but mentally very alert and a man's eyes are the mirrors of his soul. His room was a mass of papers, files and faded maps of the area. The furniture was the creation of an amateur carpenter, a combination of tea-boxes and rough wood planks tacked together with little skill or attention to spirit-levels. The only pictures on the walls were three dog-eared and much-fingered pin-ups from the 1950's. It had the feeling of being very much lived in, an extension of the man himself, his dreams and desires.

It was a big occasion for Pundanhar, not only had the convoy got through safely, but three visitors had come with it. We were the first journalists in their memory to have visited Pundanhar and we were not allowed to forget it. From having first chance with the shower, a bucket of warm water suspended precariously from the roof, to being guests of honour at the head of the table in the officers' mess. Their hospitality and warmth were overwhelming.

We were treated to a "special" meal put together by a small Portuguese soldier with an intense desire to please the company with his dexterity in transforming tinned food into a meal fit for kings. The anxiety with which he watched us eat must have made him the most dedicated cook south of the Equator. His intensity brought a frown to his forehead which etched great lines of concentration below his receding hairline. He was like a silent waif as his thin frame hurried from the primus stove to the table in an endless mercy mission. As we ate he cowered in the background wringing his hands like a 20th century Uriah Heep. As each mouthful was tasted, he watched the faces for any sign of dissatisfaction. A smack of the lips or the occasional muffled burp was like music to his ears, for on those occasions he would allow a little smile of satisfaction to break around the corners of his mouth.

The evening's conversation with these officers was a bit disturbing. One of them had been imprisoned by the DGS, formerly PIDE the Portuguese secret police, while still a student in Portugal. There was little disguised disgust for the DGS in his voice.

"They're not so bad in Mozambique because they concentrate their efforts on the war and are responsible for gathering information for the army. They act as the intelligence arm here in Mozambique and they do a useful job of work. But in Portugal they are like Gestapo because they are political police and are responsible to the Prime Minister alone. They have too much power and they are always abusing it on the people." He said the DGS could be incredibly brutal, and in Portugal people were afraid to speak their minds in case the DGS got to hear about it. There was quite a lot of underground opposition in Portugal and even among the ordinary people if the occasion ever arose, they would revenge themselves on the secret police.

Even in Mozambique the DGS had built up a type of repressive image. I had been warned on more than one occasion not to upset the sensibilities of the secret police if I ever wanted to return to Mozambique. Being responsible to no one but the now deposed Prime Minister Caetano, DGS was an unknown quantity and being responsible for gathering the information on which the army acted this security agency seemed to be wielding more real power and influence than any other single group in Mozambique, including the army.

It was believed that DGS had planned counter-insurgency into Tanzania in 1971 overriding the army which had adopted a negative attitude regarding punitive expeditions across the Tanzanian and Zambian borders as being politically explosive. The plans only came unstuck when they were finally overruled by Dr. Caetano himself in Lisbon.

In Mozambique, the DGS was openly hostile to the army's attitudes toward fighting the war. There was a DGS inspector in each of the territory's nine provinces. Most of them were ex-army captains with combat experience and with firm ideas on how the war should be conducted. Prime Minister Caetano's directive not to engage Frelimo in Tanzania was believed to have caused friction between the secret police and Caetano. Caetano's "liberal" attitude toward certain Left-wing elements in Metropolitan Portugal, notably the Communist Party, was also a bone of contention with the DGS.

Dissatisfaction came to a head in 1972 when ARA, the militant wing of the outlawed Portuguese Communist Party, destroyed eight Puma helicopters on the ground in Lisbon. The helicopters were destined for Mozambique and were desperately needed to supplement the Mozambique Air Force which was stretched to the limits.

There was no denying the DGS capabilities in Mozambique. This arm had repeatedly penetrated Frelimo security and in some cases was known to have tipped the army off days in advance of a Frelimo attack before it took place. As a security agency there was no denying its ability, but in the Mozambique I saw there were strong indications that the DGS would like to test its competance in other fields and take a more active part in the war effort.

It had already established its own para-military unit known as the Fleches (or Arrows). They began operating in the Vila Pery district, not far from the Rhodesian border, late in 1973 and had already proved themselves as formidable anti-guerrilla fighters. Their advantage lay in the fact that many of them were rehabilitated Frelimos who knew the tactics of the enemy intimately.

The mere existence of the Fleches as a military unit was an indication of how much power the DGS wielded in the inner sanctums of Government in Lisbon because as DGS took its directives from the Prime Minister alone it faced no restrictions from the army in

55

Mozambique and although there appeared to be a good working relationship between DGS and the military, it became increasingly obvious as I travelled through the territory that DGS despised its information-gathering role and wanted more power. This was disconcerting to many of the young officers, some of whom had experienced DGS power while still students in Portugal and there was a feeling that DGS and the army, although co-operating on one level, were working at cross purposes in their own power struggle. Since my first visit to Mozambique, the DGS were absorbed into the army, but when the extent of its activities became known its members were either imprisoned or hounded out of Mozambique.

As I spoke to the officers and men in Pundanhar I became increasingly aware of how well informed they were despite the total lack of news reaching the camp. They were politically aware and anxious about the future of Mozambique, but they accepted the war and the concept of a Euro-African Portugal.

As the evening wore on and the warm alcohol brought us together in our mutual experiences and companionship, the captain of the garrison asked Jimmy Soullier if he would like to shoot a gun.

"Sure," said Jimmy with characteristic enthusiasm.

"Lieutenant 'Boom-boom' here is the officer in charge," said the captain nodding toward a smiling young man his eyes twinkling behind dark-rimmed glasses. "Come we will go and shoot."

Jimmy Soullier leaned over to me and said: "Who's this Boom Boom guy – surely that's not his name?"

"No its just an example of the universality of the English language. They probably call him Boom Boom because he's the gunnery officer or something, it's an onomatopoeia."

"I wonder what they call their sanitary inspector?" quipped Jimmy as we got up to follow the lieutenant and captain.

Outside most of the men were milling about. The captain walked behind Lieutenant "Boom-boom" who paved the way with his hurricane lamp held aloft. The men filed after us in a quiet procession.

"Shooting" had sounded fine in the comfort of the officers' mess, but I had had no idea the captain was talking about an artillary piece. The howitzer I was about to shoot was of post-World War II vintage and looked like a 10-pounder. The men gathered around the sandbags while I sat on the gun's little metal seat feeling a bit apprehensive.

Lieutenant "Boom-boom" fiddled around with the range-finder. His voice was slightly slurred as he said: "Open your mouth as wide as you can before you pull the handle or you will go deaf for a few days. You will shoot 5 kilometres to the Tanzanian border."

As I jerked the handle downwards and felt the gun recoil I conjured up visions of international repercussions and frantic United Nations delegates calling for Portugal's blood for firing on innocent villages in Tanzania. As the shell exploded in the distance I looked around at all the smiling faces emerging from behind the sandbags. It was like a bizarre comedy; they were all nodding their encouragement.

Not satisfied with that performance, we all marched to the other side of the camp where another howitzer awaited Jimmy Soullier. This time Lieutenant "Boom-boom" brought the barrel right down. "You will shoot 800 metres", he told Jimmy who was already perched on the gunner's seat. No camera offered such a challenge as this.

The report from the gun and the explosion were almost simultaneous. Jimmy was still sitting on the seat, his mouth wide open and his eyes even wider. Lieutenant "Boom-boom" and the captain walked over to the 40-gallon drums in front of the gun which acted as sandbags. The sand was heaped over the drums, and in a direct line with the barrel of the gun one of the little heaps had been parted, two inches from the top of the drum. The two officers looked at the drum carefully, turned to each other and burst out laughing.

Jimmy and I didn't share their humour as we walked quietly back to the mess. For the second time in one day we had come just that bit too close to death, first Frelimo and now two fun-loving Portuguese officers with a "toy" howitzer. Jimmy probably still holds the record in Pundanhar for getting closest to the lip of the drum with that howitzer and he told me later he was quite proud of the fact.

The following morning we handed in our uniforms and my G3 automatic and drove off to the airstrip in the captain's Jeep, a Willys built in South Africa. A Berliet truck was careering up and down the runway and troops had stationed themselves at intervals down the narrow grass strip. The truck was making sure no mines had been laid on the runway overnight, which was an indication of Frelimo activity in the northern border areas where guerrilla bands had almost total freedom of movement and could come within a kilometer of a Portuguese military camp without being detected.

57

The convoy had left Pundanhar for Nicha another camp like Pundanhar about 25 kilometres to the east and five kilometres from the Tanzanian border, long before sunrise and the captain told me Lieutenant Pereira's men were at that moment repairing another truck which had exploded a mine only five kilometres from Pundanhar. That, presumably, was the reason for our hosts making sure the airstrip was clear of mines before the aircraft arrived.

The plane seemed to fall out of the sky, wasting no time in dropping to earth, landing then taxiing to a halt in front of us. The troops collected the mail and a parcel of medical supplies, bid us farewell quickly then stood back as we climbed into the aircraft. As the pilot was about to close the door, the captain walked up and handed me his camouflage cap. "I will draw another," he said, then walked back to his Jeep.

The plane took off and circled the camp gaining height before flying north then turning west to follow the Rovuma River, the early morning light glinting off its waters like a long curving mirror. My mind wandered to the men on the convoy and their unenviable task of supplying their colleagues along the border, and as we flew off to a safer spot something Lieutenant Pereira said kept recurring in my mind: "You must remember that our war here is ultimately your war in South Africa."

I know many people in South Africa who had never even given it a thought.

CHAPTER FIVE

MOZAMBIQUE'S "DA NANG": MUEDA

Portuguese development planning in the northern reaches of Cabo Delgado was in the hands of the military. An ambitious social development programme called "Operation Frontier" was underway in the area along the Mozambique border with Tanzania. It was organised like an inverted triangle, the base stretching along the Rovuma River with the apex of the triangle reaching down to Mueda, the largest frontline military camp in Cabo Delgado, and a garrison that had repeatedly been attacked by large groups of Frelimo guerrillas. The last attack before my arrival lasted only 30 minutes in which time 150 122 mm missiles hit the camp.

"Operation Frontier" was a social promotion in the Portuguese dictionary, but more correctly it was a piece of strategic military planning. Cabo Delgado had traditionally been the achilles heel of the Portuguese war effort in Mozambique. In 1964 the first group of Frelimo guerrillas crossed the Rovuma River into Cabo Delgado from Tanzania and groups have crossed that river almost at will ever since, using local recruits to act as bearers carrying arms, munitions and supplies. The Portuguese army had found no way of stopping these bands of rebels and had lost all freedom of movement in the area. The army was confined to small fortified camps some of which were constantly in danger of being attacked or even overrun.

Frelimo claims to "control" 20 per cent of Mozambique. In fact, at the time of writing Frelimo would be optimistic if they staked a claim to five per cent of the territory and that five per cent would mostly be in Cabo Delgado. In this area Frelimo could muster as many as 400 troops at any one time backed with sophisticated weapons ranging from the Russian built 122 mm missile to recoilless rockets. But this was not a war to control the land. It was a struggle for men's minds and in that department the Portuguese were losing hands down.

To try and prevent infiltration across the Rovuma River the Portuguese launched "Operation Frontier" with a dual purpose. Ostensibly the programme was to promote the wellbeing of the local population in the area, most of whom are Maconde tribesmen, whom the Portuguese considered to be 90 per cent subverted by Frelimo. But the programme was also aimed at controlling the population, bringing them into select areas where the Portuguese could prevent them liaising with the enemy.

In the centre of this development triangle is the garrison of Nangade, about 10 kilometres from the Rovuma River. Nangade is a fairly large military outpost and being so close to the Tanzanian border is a frontline defence against Frelimo. Recently the Portuguese have begun building a large aldeamento, using brick and mortar to build the houses rather than mud and straw. Almost one million rands have been injected into the scheme so far. Primary and secondary schools have been built and a technical college provides students with the facilities to develop a wide range of technical skills. Nangade is a showpiece of Portuguese development planning.

Since the coup in Portugal there has been no indication that operation frontier will not continue. Portugal has stated she will give every assistance to her three overseas provinces both to help develop them and to help them decide upon their self-determination.

But large numbers of Portuguese troops, Black and White, have defected to Frelimo and a number of the base camps in the north have been abandoned since the coup. It is unlikely the development programme will continue with Portuguese finance.

We arrived there at 10 in the morning. The heat was overpowering, burning down on the already scorched earth. Many of the troops walked about without shirts and the heat brought the sweat out on their deeply tanned shoulders. The Portuguese fighting man is unlike any other I have met. Unlike the South African or Rhodesian, he is probably the last of an old breed. He fights under singularly difficult conditions with little or no comforts and accepts his lot without questioning.

I met members of the regular army, of which there are about 60 000 in Mozambique, who had been in Mozambique for nearly four years although their period of service should only have stretched for two and a half years. The quality of the troops varies. The White troops are quite open about the fighting ability of their Black colleagues, who make up 60 per cent of the regular army in Mozambique. The Black regular troops are decidedly inferior to their White counterparts and although the army is totally integrated, there is a definite social barrier between the two ethnic groups. The White troops are an army within an army, but there is no animosity between the two. They are all treated equally.

There are also five special units attached to the Portuguese army: the GEs (Group Especial) and GEPs (Group Especial Paratroop), both volunteer units and predominantly Black troops; the Commandos, Paratroops and Marines. Seventy per cent of these troops are Black and, unlike their counterparts in the regular army, are crack soldiers making up the spearhead of the Portuguese war effort in the territory. These special units are fully operational and are air-lifted to trouble spots all over Mozambique to seek out and destroy Frelimo groups. They sometimes spend weeks in the bush tracking down guerrilla bands and their instructions are usually not to return to base unless they return with captured Frelimo weapons.

Portuguese policy was to bring captured Frelimos back to be mentally rehabilitated by DGS, the secret police, but in practice they were often shot out of hand. Portuguese soldiers who were found to have willfully killed enemy troops without making the effort to try and capture them faced prison sentences ranging up to eight years. It was a policy that caused considerable dissatisfaction among many of the special troops who argued with conviction that no quarter could be given in war if it were to be won.

There is very little formality in the Portuguese army. In the entire period I spent in Mozambique I hardly saw a single soldier salute an officer. "It isn't that there is no respect for officers, simply that there is no place for British square-bashing routine and formality in the bush. We keep that for the training bases," was how an instructor explained it. He may have had a point. Very different from, say, the British attitude to bush fighting in earlier campaigns.

It was only one hundred years ago that the British found themselves fighting a fierce and humiliating campaign against the Ashanti in the West African territory of the Gold Coast. It was during this campaign that the first instructions for jungle warfare were drawn up by General Sir Garnett Wolseley, "the very model of a modern major-general".

Before that the approach to war was like something out of musical comedy except that the "cast" were culpably sacrificed through ignorance and lack of imagination.

It makes Wolseley's appreciation of the needs all the more interesting and I am indebted to Alan Lloyd who quotes Garnett Wolseley's pamphlet in his excellent book on the Ashanti wars,

"The Drums of Kumasi" (Longmans) for the following details.

Wolseley had fought in Burma twenty years earlier as a subaltern. The experience of wandering through the jungle in sweltering heat clad in a scarlet jacket buttoned to the chin, tight trousers and white buckskin gloves left a deep impression on his mind. His memory of the discomfort caused him to arrange something more suitable for his Ashanti campaign.

His instructions to his men, issued in pamphlet form to all regiments, paved the way for modern army methods in bush warfare. They were exceptional in the stress laid on individual independence of action for small groups of men and on individual initiative.

"The officers must see that tea or chocolate, with a little biscuit, is provided for their men every morning before marching, and quinine will be served out by the medical orderlies.

"During the heat of the day, or when marching late in the morning, commanding officers may, at their discretion, allow the patroljackets to be taken off and carried by the men. These can be easily carried slung behind under the waistbelt. Immediately when the march is over, of if any long halt takes place, these jackets must be put on;for a chill, when the body is heated, is above all things to be avoided.

"The following maxims should be impressed on the men:
1. Never allow the body to suffer from a chill, and there will not be much chance of your ever being sick.
2. Never expose the head uncovered to the sun; and when halting, or on sentry, get into the shade if possible.
3. When camping for the night, do your best to construct a raised sleeping place, even a few inches off the ground.
4. If any irregularity of the bowels is experienced, go at once to the doctor for a dose.
5. Never drink water until you have filtered it.

"Mode of fighting: The theatre of operations will be a great forest of gigantic trees, with an undergrowth of bush varying in thickness. At some places men can get through the bush in skirmishing order, at others they will have to use their sword-bayonets to open paths for themselves. All the fighting will be in skirmishing order, the files being two, three or four paces apart, according to circumstances.

"When once thus engaged in a fight in the bush, officers commanding battalions, and even officers commanding companies, will find it difficult to exercise much control over their men. For this reason it is essential that the tactical unit should be as small as possible. Every company will therefore be at once divided into four sections, and each section will be placed under the command of an officer or non-commissioned officer. These sections, once told off, are not on any account to be broken up during the war, nor are their commanders to be changed except under extraordinary circumstances, and then only by order of the officer commanding the battalion.

"In action, as a general rule, three sections only of each company will be extended, and the fourth will form a support in rear of the centre of the company's skirmishing line, and at from 40 to 80 yards from it. Care must be taken that the support never loses sight of its own skirmishers, and that it conforms to their movements; but its commander must never allow it to become mixed up with the skirmishers, unless it be ordered forward by the officer commanding the company. The captain will always be with the skirmishing line exercising a general control over it; and as the enemy only fight in loose skirmishing order, it will seldom be necessary to bring forward support into the skirmishing line.

"Fighting in the bush is very much like fighting in the twilight; no one can see further than a few files to his right or left. Great steadiness and self-confidence are therefore required from everyone engaged. The Ashantis always employ the same tactics. Being superior in numbers, they encircle their enemy's flanks by long lines of skirmishers, hoping thereby to demoralise their opponents. The men engaged in our front lines should not concern themselves about these flank attacks. They must have the same confidence in their general that he has in them, and depend on him to take the necessary measures for meeting all such attacks whether in flank or rear. Each soldier must remember that with his breech-loader he is equal to at least twenty Ashantis, wretchedly armed as they are with old flint-muskets, firing slugs or pieces of stone that do not hurt badly at more than 40 or 50 yards range. Our enemies have neither guns nor rockets, and have a superstititious dread of those used by us.

"In action, the two comrades forming each file must always keep together, and the officers and non-commissioned officers commanding sections will use their utmost endeavours to keep their sections from mixing up with those on their left and right.

"If during the advance through the bush, fire is unexpectedly opened by the enemy concealed behind cover, the men will immediately drop on the knee behind trees or any cover that may be at hand, pausing well before delivering their fire, and taking care to fire low at the spots from which the enemy were seen to fire. All firing against a concealed enemy should be very slow, and officers and non-commissioned officers in command of sections must spare no efforts to prevent the men from wasting their ammunition.

"The advance will be made along narrow paths, where the men can only march in file, and sometimes only in single file; when an action commences, the troops on the centre path will deploy to the front into skirmishing order, either to the right or left of the path as ordered, on the leading file; the rear section of each company will always form the support, and officers commanding companies will be careful to lead these deployments so that their front may always be as nearly as possible at right angles to the path they had been marching on. All officers must remember that the front line will, a sa general rule, face north by west, and when at any distance from the path, they must guide the direction of their advance by compass.

"Officers commanding battalions and companies will not order any bugle-call to be sounded in camp or on the march, except to repeat those sounded on the main road by order of the major-general commanding; and these, if preceded by any special regimental call, will be repeated only by the battalion concerned, and by any battalion that may be operating between the main road and the corps indicated by the call. When any call is not preceded by a regimental call, it will be repeated by every bugler within hearing, except those that may be on duty with the baggage-guard.

"Whenever the advance or double is sounded, it is understood to order a general advance of the whole front line on the enemy. The men will then advance cheering at a fast walk, making short rushes whenever the nature of the ground will allow of their being made. All such advances will be preceded by a heavy force of guns and rockets.

"On reaching a clearing in the course of the action, or when the enemy is in the immediate neighbourhood, the troops will not cross over the open space until the clearing has been turned and the bush on both sides of it has been occupied.

"When once a position has been gained, it is to be held resolutely. In warfare of this nature there must be no retreats.

"No village or camp is to be set on fire except by order of the major-general commanding. Officers and men are reminded of the

Left: General Basto Machado, former chief of the armed forces in Mozambique. The general, described as "a quiet, but solid soldier" was fired soon after the Movement of the Armed Forces took command in Portugal.

—Picture: James Soullier.

Right: General Diogo Neto, the flamboyant former chief of the Mozambique Air-force. General Neto was to become No. 3 in Spinola's military junta that ruled Portugal after the coup.

—Picture: James Soullier.

General Spinola, the intellectual soldier turned politician in whose hands the future of Portugal and her three African provinces rest.—Picture: Courtesy United Press International.

danger and delay which occur if a village is set on fire before all the ammunition and baggage have made their way through it.

"All plundering and unnecessary destruction of property are to be strictly repressed. Officers are held responsible that when a village or camp is occupied their men are kept together, and prevented from dispersing to seek plunder.

"The importance of kindness from all ranks to the friendly natives who are employed as carriers cannot be too strongly urged. If the carriers are ill-treated the troops run imminent risk of being left without food and ammunition.

"It must never be forgotten by our soldiers that Providence has implanted in the heart of every native of Africa a superstitious awe and dread of the White man that prevents the Negro from daring to meet us face to face in combat. A steady advance or charge, no matter how partial, if made with determination, always means the retreat of the enemy. Although when at a distance, and even when under heavy fire, the Ashantis seem brave enough, from their practice of yelling, and singing, and beating drums, in order to frighten the enemies of their own colour, with whom they are accustomed to make war, they will not stand against the advance of the White man.

"Soldiers and sailors remember that the Black man holds you in superstitious awe; be cool; fire low; fire slow, and charge home; the more numerous your enemy the greater will be the loss inflicted on him, and the greater your honour in defeating him."

But Garnett Wolseley's incredible document, which was the first recorded attempt at formulating methods of countering the African on his home ground, was revolutionary. At least in one campaign Wolseley changed the British soldier from a peacock to a bush fighter. A little earlier on the Gold Coast officers went into battle in the dense bush wearing fulldress uniform, including plumes. One such officer ended up with his skull being used as a drinking vessel by the wild Ashantis. The Ashanti campaign was reported by none other than Stanley, the man who eventually found Livingstone before the emaciated and desperately ill adventurer moved on to Tete in Mozambique on his overland trudge from Angola to the Indian Ocean.

Today Wolseley's instructions are laughable and in Africa's silent guerrilla campaigns the actual military struggle has become of secondary importance. It was Mao Tse-tung who wrote: "The people

65

are to the guerrilla fighter as water is to the fish" and as Portugal moves into nearly 14 years of guerrilla struggle in Africa Mao's words never seem more profound than today. Nangade is a symbol of Portuguese tactics in her war in Mozambique for it is in Nangade that the army is trying to win the fierce Maconde tribesmen to Portuguese thinking on a multiracial Mozambique under the wing of Portugal.

The next stop on our journey through the north was at Mueda, the shell-shocked military capital of Cabo Delgado. Mueda is a military stronghold perched on the top of a plateau like a self-contained armoury in the sky. To the north and west of Mueda runs an even valley with the occasional deep green hill protruding from the valley floor like a lonely sentinel. From the periphery of the camp you can look out over the valley and on clear days to the west the tiny camp of Chamba is just visible in the thick jungle that envelopes the valley like a hovering cloud of green and deeper green, a sea of trees swimming all around without a shade of difference in the monotonous colour scheme.

Mueda is the military springboard to Cabo Delgado. The camp is a strong-point housing the largest group of regular troops in the north and is also the Air Force headquarters of Cabo Delgado.

Although we were staying with the colonel commanding Mueda and basked in his generous hospitality, our guide and companion was a second lieutenant called Carlos Lucas. Carlos was from Lisbon and had been serving his tour of duty in Mueda as the commanding officer of a crack group of volunteer GE troops. He was worshipped by his men all of whom were Black and most of whom had been with him for the entire period of his command. Carlos was well built and he kept in constant training for operations in the bush. He had a wide, generous mouth and a quick sense of humour which turned out to be far too subtle for either his men or many of the other officers who shared his life in Mueda. Consequently, this officer latched himself on to any visitors to the camp with open curiosity and alert mind. Like many officers in Mozambique, he was curious for news of the war position in the territory and was puzzled by the high command's methods of conducting the war.

"You may not believe this," he said one afternoon as we made our way to a point outside the camp where a month previously a group of 100 Frelimo guerrillas had attacked the camp's water installations.

"I have spent most of my time in the jungle with my men. On more than one occasion we have captured the same Frelimo twice. There was one guy we caught four times before I shot him. I'm not saying that this always happens, but many of the Frelimos that we take in the bush and hand over to the authorities for mental rehabilitation simply return to the Frelimos the moment they are released. It has a bad psychological effect on the men who risk their lives to bring Frelimos back and I can tell you more and more groups are not taking prisoners any longer."

This point was brought home even more strongly by an incident he related to me later in the day. We were in the Maconde section of Mueda's aldeamento watching some of the residents carving the "Maconde Christ", a stylised crucifix with long delicate hands and feet for which the Maconde carvers are famous throughout Mozambique. In my opinion the Maconde carvers are among the most imaginative in Africa.

Carlos said: "Look, forget them, I will give you mine. It was carved by a man who was the best carver in Cabo Delgado. He used to be attached to my unit when he wasn't drunk. Now he is in prison.

"We found that all the money he was making from his carvings was being sent straight to Frelimo so we had no option but to imprison him."

The man he was referring to was known as Roberto and to my knowledge he is still in prison for his trouble. In the little church in Mueda, one of Roberto's Christs, a beautiful piece of work a full six-foot tall, hangs at the head of the altar, its face a portrait of agony and intense suffering. The carving Carlos gave me in exchange for a few cold beers in the officers' mess now hangs on my wall in Johannesburg as a reminder of the "Black Judas" who carved it in Mueda.

Mueda represents a symbol to Frelimo and although they were unable to overrun the well-fortified camp, large groups of guerrillas have launched a number of attacks on the garrison. The previous month a band of 100 Frelimos attacked the water installations, a barbed wire fortification about one kilometer outside Mueda's fences.

The twisting road that runs out to the camp's water supply is flanked by high elephant grass merging into bush about 30 metres off the road. Interspersed in the shoulder-high grass is the occasional tree and anthill which the busy African termite builds like miniature Towers of Pisa, which lean every which way and seem to mock man's vast concrete buildings that often deface the skylines of cities throughout the world. It was the great South African poet and author, Eugéne Marais, who compared the African anthill to the human body, a single living organism that is like any other of nature's animals except that its organs are loosely connected and can function outside the animal's body. Marais's findings were plagiarised by a Belgian called Maeterlink who published Marais's work as his own and won a Nobel Prize. The shock was too much for the sensitive Afrikaans poet, already a morphine addict. The shattered old man denied humanity further insight to his wonderfully sensitive mind by committing suicide. The African anthill, however, will remain as Marais's monument to posterity long after many concrete domes and fenced-in parks have disappeared.

The bullet holes arched across the concrete tower and punctured the thin metal skins of the three water towers. The Frelimo group had attacked the installation at first light raking it with machinegun fire. Only four Portuguese soldiers were defending it and for close on an hour they returned the fire with their rifles.

Hearing the shooting in the distance, the duty troops in Mueda jumped into their trucks and drove out to the water installations. The trucks were ambushed on the way, only a few metres outside Mueda's fence by a heavily armed group of Frelimos lying in the thick grass flanking the road. They were eventually driven off, but not without loss. Incidents like these have left Mueda in a constant state of alertness.

Throughout Mueda you can see evidence of missile attacks where the 122 mm missiles have dropped on the area. These attacks sometimes last as long as two hours and are usually launched between four pm and seven. The 122 mm missile is the latest piece of weaponry used by Frelimo. It is only used in the north because of the difficulty in transporting the weapon and its steel ramp through the bush. It has a tremendous concussion that blows windows out at distances up to 800 metres and the crater it leaves is often six feet deep and equally as wide. The weapon has had more of a psychological impact on the Portuguese than any destructive capability. The men's mess suffered a direct hit by one of these missiles. One of the walls collapsed and the roof was blown right off the building, but no deaths resulted as the men were still on duty. If the missile had hit the mess during a meal, half of Mueda's defenders would have been wiped out.

The 122 mm missile, however, is also a liability to Frelimo. Because it requires ramp firing, it has to be fired from a clearing in the jungle which gives Portuguese air reconnaisance a chance to detect the attackers. When this happens, and it does with increasing regularity as the Portuguese familiarise themselves with the possible areas from which the missiles can be launched, the Fiat jets and Harvard T6 bombers stationed at Mueda can counter-attack from the air within minutes.

This was the case during the attack on Nangade when 150 missiles hit the camp in 30 minutes. The Fiat jets were scrambled from Mueda. One sighted the clearing where six missile ramps were sited. The pilot attacked, guns blazing and dropped his two bombs on the clearing. The following morning a ground patrol found the clearing. All six ramps had been destroyed and the Portuguese estimated 35 guerrillas died at the spot although it was difficult to judge accurately as some of the bodies had been blown to bits in the air attack.

The weapon is also cumbersome to carry and Frelimo groups have to recruit large numbers of bearers to carry the weapons in any quantity into Mozambique. Bearers can also be a liability to the highly trained guerrillas as they are largely undisciplined and many of them are forced to act as bearers at gunpoint.

Also in Mueda is one of the most sophisticated mechanical workshops in Mozambique. Here all the badly damaged vehicles are repaired by an expert team of mechanics who often work around the clock to get the vehicles back into service. The workshops suffered a direct hit recently by a Russian recoilless rocket which passed through the roof and impacted itself in the back wall of the spares depot attached to the workshops before exploding. The officer commanding the workshops has refused to have the damage repaired as a reminder to his mechanics that they are frontline soldiers and as such must maintain a constant sense of urgency in their vital work.

Like air force units throughout the world, the section of the Mozambique Air Force stationed at Mueda is a world within a world. The pilots' mess has a sense of quiet efficiency about it while retaining the intimacy that characterises most airmen's surroundings. The pilots are carefree in company, but brooding alone. Their duties

69

range from transport and supply to those of the crack fighter pilots who fly the Fiat jets on strike missions throughout the north. Among these men, however, the helicopter pilots are a breed apart. It is their unenviable task to evacuate the wounded from the jungle and fly them back to the base hospitals.

"You have to harden yourself," said a stocky young chopper pilot who had been in Mueda for nearly a year. His dark sensuous face creased as he continued: "The first evacuation I flew set the pattern for me. I flew out with a gunboat to protect my landing. As he hovered above firing into the bush, I saw the ground troops lying in a circle around the fringe of the clearing.

"I dropped down as quickly as possible and they brought the injured man across. Both his legs had been taken off below the knee and although unconscious he was crying, the tears rolling down his cheeks drawing uneven furrows through the dust and sweat on his face. We laid him across the back seat strapping him down as best we could. Then a guy ran from the bush holding a parcel made up of a blood-stained camouflage jacket. He put it down on the floor and ran off. I watched it slide open. It held the mutilated torso of a dead soldier and part of his decapitated head which rolled drunkenly out of the package onto the floor. I was violently ill and it took me a few minutes before I could take off and fly back to base.

"But that's changed now. I have forced myself to feel nothing for the men I fly out of the bush. If my feelings took over I wouldn't be able to do my job and would probably lose my own life in the process.

"The only time I feel anything is when I fly an injured Frelimo out of the bush while our own injured have to stay and wait for the next chopper. If there's space for only one man, we have to evacuate an injured Frelimo before our own men. If the injured man is far from base and his wounds are bad, by the time we return to pick him up his wounds are infected and he has less chance of pulling through."

His face twitched as he told me this as if he wanted to tear out some of the hidden memories and display them to me, to force me to understand his state of mind and the agonies he underwent in controlling his anger at Portuguese military policy regarding the evacuation of wounded.

On the face of it this may seem strange, but the Portuguese have been determined through these methods to give the lie to Frelimo propaganda that the Portuguese never take prisoners. In fact, they do far more. Captured guerrillas are given preference and share the same beds as injured Portuguese troops in the military hospitals. The war in Mozambique is the war for people's minds and the Portuguese attempt to rehabilitate captured Frelimos before recruiting them for the Portuguese forces or giving them positions in the running of the territory.

As with most outlying military camps, much of the talk centres around the war and women. In Mueda's African quarter you can see the occasional "child of the escudo", light-skinned and the obvious product of an interracial union. They are freely accepted by the residents despite their loveless beginnings. But not many of the men cohabit with African women, and during my stay in Mueda I think I found out the reason why.

"After supper we will visit the brothel," said Carlos Lucas, our self-appointed guardian. We were sitting in the officers' mess sipping "chicken soup", which turned out to be a tasteless mixture of rice and water. Vegetables are often impossible to come by in Mueda as in much of Mozambique. The Portuguese have one thing in common with the Irish in their love of potatoes, but the only time they get them is when a South African transport flies into Mueda with food, which is not a common occurrence, although 137 tons of food were flown into Mueda by South African transport planes last year.

Carlos's decision to visit Mueda's brothel broke the monotony of the conversation which had centred around the war most of the afternoon and I decided to play along.

"Where is it?" I asked.

"At the hospital," said Carlos. My interest was aroused even further.

After the meal, we walked the darkened streets; past the little chapel, the officers' quarters and through the gate to the hospital. An ambulance drove past and disappeared round a bend in the road. From the jungle beyond the fence I heard the night beating its primitive sounds, and above the Southern Cross rose resplendent in the night sky, its image stretched to heaven, a fantasy of roving stars and tinselled planets. The February moon looked down with an approving smile, a cosmic benediction for the careless warriors below. I felt carefree and heady.

Like three thieves in the night we entered the hospital's west wing through a back door and were met there by a White attendant, his overall opened at the front, the lined jacket flapping about his knees. Carlos said something to him in Portuguese. The attendant looked us over, gave us a knowing nod then turned on his heel and walked down the long corridor. I was already conjuring up visions of voluptuous Portuguese nurses that soon turned into sun-tanned girls on Cape Town's Clifton Beach, their bikinis heaving beneath the pressures of form placed upon them. As we followed Carlos and his attendant friend down the long corridor, it didn't require much imagination to take the next logical mental step.

We turned a corner and the attendant selected a key from a bunch he pulled out of his pocket, opened a door and switched on the light. We followed timidly. Selecting another key from his bunch, he went to an interleading door. We entered and Carlos closed the door behind us. We had arrived.

It was a tiny room with the distinct smell of carbolic soap hanging in the air. One small window looked out into the darkness. There was a wooden bed in one corner and a cupboard in the other. On the floor was a small portable hi-fi and four records. Carlos sat down on the bed and we followed suit as the attendant took yet another key and opened the cupboard. I somehow expected my visions to come out of the cupboard, mouths pouting, breasts heaving. Instead, the attendant brought out a tattered portfolio and dexterously opened it. Inside was a pile of Playboy centrespreads. "He also sells pornography," said Carlos, "but only to look, not to have."

Despite myself, I burst out laughing. The attendant looked hurt, but soon we all joined in and I congratulated the medic on his business acumen. And that's how we ended up the evening, surrounded by Playboy centrespreads, sipping wine in a close fellowship.

CHAPTER SIX

GENERAL BASTO MACHADO: NAMPULA

We left Mueda the following morning. Vast storm clouds were billowing over the plateau on to the valley below, shutting out the morning sun and leaving everything bathed in a bright metallic light that highlighted the matt colourings of camouflage on the airbase buildings. Everything had changed; the jungle valley was covered with a dizzy grey glare and on the base pastel shades of light blue and dull pink reflected off the buildings as if some sad painter had dipped into Nature's paintbox and festooned the morning with the secret colours of a solitary mourner.

Seconds after takeoff the twin-engined Aero-Commander was through the cloud base, buffetted about like a tiny fishing boat in a stormy sea. Flashes of lightning stabbed past the cockpit, illuminating the pilot's face into what looked like a death mask with lines of concentration etched into his brow as he put all his effort into the nervy job of flying the aircraft.

The pilot was Machado Da Cruz; fairly tall, thin, well-groomed, sunglasses hooked into the front of his short-sleeved shirt and long strong fingers deftly manipulating the controls as the aircraft dipped and soared like a paper kite.

Before take-off from Mueda, I had spoken briefly to Machado about the risks the commercial pilots take in flying the air taxies in Cabo Delgado. He was warm and friendly, easy to communicate with. We were the same age, 24, but he seemed like a wise old man, especially when at the controls where he was one up on me. In the pilot's seat he was the boss – and looked it, despite the gentler and more apparent aspects of his character.

My first impression of him was of a mercenary; he had that happy-go-lucky look about him and I liked him immediately. His face was thin but open with an acquiline nose, perhaps a bit too sharp to be handsome. His tall, thin frame seemed to glide rather than walk around, and I noticed how popular he was with the other airmen in Mueda.

Three weeks after our harrowing flight from Mueda to Porto Amelia, a natural harbour about 300 kilometres south of the Tanzanian border, I learnt of Machado's death. He had told me how on two occasions he had been fired at from the ground; once by small arms, once by a Frelimo anti-aircraft battery concealed in the jungle below. It was third time unlucky for Machado. There were conflicting reports about his death. Some said he had developed engine trouble while flying to evacuate an injured Portuguese soldier from Mueda, but I learnt on a later visit to Mozambique that he had been brought down by Frelimo ground fire. He was last heard radioing back to base that he was being shot at from the jungle below. Moments later the radio was silent and the broken body of the young pilot was found lying in the burnt-out wreckage of his twin-engined Aero-Commander in the jungle of Cabo Delgado. But I remember him as he was before, an airman who loved his work and disregarded the dangers to fly his mercy missions in the north. That, I am sure, is how he would prefer to be remembered for there is a strange banality in violent death that could do no man credit.

Porto Amelia was just a short stopover on our journey back to Nampula, the military headquarters of Mozambique. We had to return to Porto Amelia to drop off Jorge Martino, our interpreter friend, and catch a connecting flight to Nampula, 400 kilometres to the south. It was in Porto Amelia that a particular incident marred our journey through Mozambique. We took our leave of Machado, the pilot, at the airport and drove into the town. It was early afternoon, but seemed like night as the storm we had flown through had followed us and was buffeting the town, already hardly distinguishable through the sheets of rain.

Porto Amelia can only be described in terms of potentials. It has all the makings of a throbbing commercial centre and tourist attraction, but through lack of capital and because of the war, it has become little more than a bush stopover.

Pemba Bay, where the harbour is situated, has the potential for a large harbour, but only about 12 medium-sized ships are handled by its docks each month. It is rumoured that during World War II German U-boats recharged their batteries in the bay at night and took on supplies from sympathisers among the local population. From the docks the town climbs up to the higher ground above, where because of the incline, some of the streets are linked by flights of steps. Despite its retarded development, Porto Amelia has some of the best beaches in Mozambique and its waters yield a harvest of fish.

Jorge Martino was given a hero's welcome by the clerks in his office. He described his experiences in the north with a certain flamboyance that left his colleagues asking questions about mines and missiles. It was definitely Jorge's moment of glory, and it seemed as though there was envy in the non-combatants' voices; a score of Walter Mittys in uniform; soldiers in a war area. But it's difficult to become a hero or to win a valour award handling personnel files instead of a machinegun.

Jorge left us to report back to his commanding officer. We sat in the back of the Jeep, the rain falling about us with a steady determination to creep through the canvas roof and soak us to the skin. We sat there smoking and talking quietly for what seemed like hours before a dejected Jorge came out of the office and walked slowly over to join us. The rain formed little driblets of water on his dark face then rolled down to trickle off his nose and chin.

"I hope you won't be mad," said Jorge, looking first at Jimmy Soullier and then at me. "The officer says you will have to pay for all the flights we took in the north. I'm sorry. I will try to talk to him again, but I don't think he will listen."

I hadn't realised the Portuguese army was that hard up, and my initial reaction was one of anger. I saw Jimmy's face explode with a similar emotion. As an Aussie, his first reaction was that we were being conned, and if there's anything an Aussie hates it's being "taken", although there seem to be plenty of Australians around the globe quite capable of reversing the roles.

"That's ridiculous," I said. "You can tell the officer we're not paying a cent. If we were chartering those flights, what was the admiral of the navy doing in our plane or all those other odd bods who hitched rides with us? Besides, we're not paying to ferry the army's supplies and mail." My mind was wandering to the boxes of supplies and postbags that filled the aircraft's baggage space on each flight we made.

"Ask your officer if he wants us to pay for the lift we had on the fighting convoy from Palma," added Jimmy. We were too tired and to angry to be tactful.

Jorge was embarrassed, but, he started the Jeep and we drove into the town in silence, the rain still hammering away at the canvas hood.

At the hotel Jorge left us, but an hour later he returned. He was washed and shaved and looked a different person. He was also dressed in civilian clothes.

"I'm sorry this happened," he said, as we sat on the bed drinking coffee. "I hope it won't spoil our friendship." Jimmy and I had surmised by this stage that the officer concerned was only trying to make a bit of money out of our ignorance. We had decided not to pay regardless of the consequences even if it meant arrest or being thrown out of Mozambique.

When we hurriedly left Porto Amelia the next day, nothing had been resolved, the "bill" wasn't paid and the only real loser was Jorge who had to face his senior officer, presumably the same one who had assigned him to the task of accompanying us on the convoy. I learnt later that nothing more was said about the incident, which only lent emphasis in my mind to the belief that the officer concerned was acting on his own initiative and not following regulations. Nice work, if you can get away with it!

A letter from Jorge weeks later said simply: "No trouble and no more convoys with mad journalists – thank God!" But the incident left a bad taste in my mouth more because Jorge had been compromised than because of the incident itself.

We flew on to Nampula, the military headquarters of Mozambique, where I was to interview the commander-in-chief of the Mozambique armed forces, General Basto Machado. Rather than face the comic extravagance of a few nights in the Hotel Portugal and on a matter of principle after our previous experiences in the place, we booked into a boarding house nearby.

The room was dirty and run down, the sink, which only had a cold water tap, gurgled through the night like an off-key trombone, and the cockroaches scurried about the room on their missions to find and accumulate more dirt. The first floor, where we were garretted, had two showers, both temperamental and awash with the body care of the other residents. The two toilets were indescribable and best left that way, and to top it off meals consisted of greasy chips, eggs, homemade sausage and green tomatoes. I'd say minus three stars in the Michelin Guide.

It did have two redeeming features: Alfredo and Said, the two blacker-than-coal odd-job men who seemed to spend every hour of the day and night trying to keep the showers in working order. But not even those two gallants ventured near the toilets and I could hardly blame them.

They were a Rosencrantz and Guildenstein combination, forever knocking on the door to bring some new comfort: a ragged foot towel, a handful of paper napkins and, on one occasion, the promise of "pretty girls". Alfredo had the most alluring smile I have ever seen – his face seemed to be all teeth in a mask of black boot polish. Said, on the other hand, was dour and formal and a bit embarrassed by Alfredo's forwardness. Together they made a great pair, and I wondered what they did in their spare time.

We left the boarding house before Alfredo and Said did some damage to themselves in their eagerness to please and before we contracted typhoid or whatever it was lurking in the dirt and squalor of the place.

Just near the Monte Carlo, a neat little pension where we finally got a room with a shower that worked, is the Marisqueira Restaurant, which serves the best sea-food in Nampula. There one evening we met a member of a commando unit, whom I shall call Antonio. We were dining on the profit I had just made on a little currency transaction with a local taxi-driver. I felt little conscience in charging him 50 escudos for the rand because he had quite blatently taken us on a joy ride around Nampula instead of taking us directly to the Monte Carlo that morning. The Mosaic Law – an eye for an eye – is a good code for a tourist and one I adopted without scruples in Mozambique, where many people in all walks of life seemed engaged in various forms of extra-mural private enterprise.

Antonio was due for release from the army after nearly four years' service with the special forces, the elite fighting troops of the Mozambique army.

He didn't quite look the part. His camouflage uniform was a bit too big for his lean frame and sagged at the knees and elbows. He had a Roman nose, much like a Maconde carving, giving his profile a semi-circular look, more like a caricature of an old-time pawnbroker than a fighting soldier. But his eyes were quite expressionless and dull. It wasn't only the drink. They were encrusted with a bitterness I had rarely seen before and his mouth was small and cruel.

We sat talking to him over a bottle of Gatao, dry white wine, which soon turned into a second and a third. As the night wore on and the prawn shells climbed higher on our plates, Antonio fished inside his little leather handbag, a customary article among the men in Mozambique, and brought out what at first looked like two dates. On closer inspection I saw they were shrunken human ears that had been neatly severed from two heads.

"What are they?" I asked.

"Ears," said Antonio fondling them in his right hand. "I cut them off Frelimos we killed in the jungle."

"But what will you do with them?"

"Keep them as souvenirs. I might also sell them in Lourenco Marques."

Antonio told us how the ears had been carefully treated in alcohol for four months and then with Johnsons Baby Powder for a further four months. He compounded the shock quality of the occasion by producing an index finger treated in the same fashion. It had a little gold chain attached.

"What's it for?" asked Jimmy.

"Key ring," said Antonio. We didn't have to ask about the next item he brought out of that grisly handbag. It was a Black man's scrotum with a zipper attached. Antonio used it as a money purse.

"It's no good bringing Frelimos back from the jungle, they will only go back and kill more people and lay more mines. So we kill them instead. In Cabo Delgado we shoot anything that moves in the jungle. It is better to shoot first and ask afterwards," said Antonio.

We finished the wine off on a sombre note. Much of the liveliness of our earlier conversation had been lost and Antonio had lapsed into his memories. There is a great deal of truth in the notion that man's basic nature comes out through drink. Antonio's had and it was not entirely pleasant to watch. Yet one could only feel sorry for him; a young, semi-educated man thrown into the brutalities of a guerrilla war. He had little desire to fight and the conflict had turned him into the man sitting before us; a lonely, troubled human being debased by circumstance, a man who had left his smiles back in Portugal, a man who had done a bad swop of hopes and beliefs for despair and disillusionment. There are a lot of Antonios knocking around.

One of the proven tragedies of war from Macedon to Mozambique is that warring nations make a virtue of killing and teach their sons how best to kill, take a pride in that competence, yet when peace comes the soldiers are expected to fall back into a slot determined for them by rules and regulations, laws and sanctions as if nothing unusual had happened. The strangest anomaly of war is peace for when the fighting ends the mental battles only begin and it is something the warring politicians have much to answer for – the spiritual corruption of countless generations.

Near the Marisqueira Restaurant is the Cathedral de Nossa Senhora da Conseicao, better known irreverantly in Nampula as "Gina Lollobrigida" because of the two well-rounded cupolas that rest on its roof. This was the home of the Bishop of Nampula, Bishop Vieira Pinto, who two weeks after my visit was deported from Mozambique, along with a few of his priests, and sent back to Lisbon.

The Bishop was suspected of inciting the local Blacks in his far-flung diocese, which stretched from Mozambique Island, north-east of Nampula, to Antonio Enes, 150 kilometres south along the coast. Two months previously, it was claimed the bishop had told a Black congregation in Lunga, near Mozambique Island, to rise with arms and throw the White men out, something that hardly endeared the Catholic bishop to the White residents in the area. When the story filtered back to Nampula the residents wanted his blood and he was probably recalled as much for his own safety as for his outspoken beliefs.

A pilot friend of mine told the strange story of the bishop and his little entourage's departure from Nampula on the first leg of their journey back to Lisbon.

"The aircraft was parked in the Air Force base because the crowds at the airport probably would have stoned it if it were near the terminal. It was a six-seater and the bishop and five priests were escorted to it safely before the angry crowd knew what was happening. Then another priest climbed into the plane and was kneeling in the aisle begging the pilot to let him go as well. He was terrified of the demonstrators outside.

"'Only 60 kilos and no baggage', he kept saying to the pilot, but it would have been unsafe to take an extra passenger. The pilot didn't need to take him out because the other priests threw him out of the plane themselves where he was left to the mercy of the crowds. They didn't show much and the man was beaten up quite badly by the demonstrators. It makes you wonder about the nature of Christian charity," said my pilot friend.

The bishop's escape from Nampula was timely, and a measure of the rage generated among a certain section of the population was the statement made to me by some White residents who said they would attack the bishop physically if ever he set foot again in Nampula.

The Portuguese have had problems with the clergy in Mozambique. In Cabo Delgado they had to close the missions and move the priests out because, it was claimed, a number of them were assisting Frelimo guerrilla bands. It is considered one of the strange anomolies of the war in Mozambique that some of the Catholic priests, especially in the north, have helped Frelimo, an organisation with communist influence from the weapons it uses to the rhetoric it repeats. Many Whites consider the only possible explanation is that the priests are either political agents hiding behind the frock, which seems unlikely, or that stories and evidence of Portuguese atrocities have reached them from their flocks and influenced them in their loyalties to Catholic Portugal. It is thought possible there was a bit of both.

The time had arrived for my interview with the commander-in-chief of the Mozambique armed forces, General Basto Machado. I considered it a priority as this introverted general had only granted one interview to the Press since taking over command in Mozambique and that to the London *Daily Telegraph*. Unlike his predecessor, General Kaulza De Arriaga, who spoke perhaps a bit too freely to the Press for his own good, General Machado was publicity shy, which to me made him all the more interesting.

The general was of medium height and delicately built. In his greygreen uniform with three stars on each shoulder glinting from a red eppulette, he was the most unlikely general one could imagine. Sallow face with glasses and warm eyes that had an almost apologetic look as he stood up to greet us from behind his desk. He looked tired and frail. The office was very small and nondescript; on the floor a well-worn carpet, on the wall behind his desk a portrait of the now exiled Prime Minister, Dr Marcello Caetano. His office overlooked the courtyard where the Portuguese flag fluttered on the end of one of the flagpoles signalling the general's presence. Below it was a military policeman lounging against the sentry box with little regard for disciplined appearance.

General Machado gave me a feeling of intimacy I have rarely experienced on formal occasions. The jacket and tie I was wearing seemed inappropriate and the officers who fluttered around in the

Samora Machel, the current president of Frelimo. He is destined to play a large part in the future of Mozambique. Picture: Courtesy Camera Press London.

Dr. Eduardo Mondlane, president of Frelimo up to his assassination in Dar-es-Salaam. Never has Mozambique needed a man like Mondlane as much as today.—Picture: Courtesy *Sunday Times*.

The first picture of Portugal's seven-man military junta. Standing left to right: General Diogo Neto; Capt. of Frigata Rosa Coutinho; Crnl. Galvao de Melo. Seated: General Costa Gomez; General Antonio de Spinola; Vice-Admiral Pinheiro de Azevado and General Jaime Silverio Marques.—Picture Courtesy United Press International.

background seemed an unlikely company for this warm and modest man.

I put my questions to him formally. I think he was actually a little nervous. The interview took the form of question and answer.

Q. General, Frelimo's thrust to the south is causing considerable speculation outside the country. Are Frelimo attacks in the Beira area an indication that a southern warfront has been opened in the area?

A. The expression "southern warfront" is not the most accurate one to describe the actions lately carried out by Frelimo in the Beira district. As you know, in this kind of war, there is neither a front nor a rearguard. It will be more correct to say that the enemy in its attempt to bring subversion to the whole Mozambique territory, tries to expand its activity in the Beira district, which is not even difficult, since it has been operating for several years in the neighbouring district of Tete.

Q. Is there any physical threat to tourists visiting Beira by rail or road?

A. In this kind of war, we cannot give absolute assurance that there is no danger on a road or railway line; especially in the border strip where the terrain, for instance, is very rough and offers good possibilities of action to the enemy.

However, a certain number of measures are under way, aimed at increasing the safety of whoever uses those communication lines.

Q. With no hope in sight of Frelimo's financial assistance being cut off, do you think the Portuguese Forces can still win the war in Mozambique?

A. As I have had the opportunity to state once before, I remain realistic about the probable evolution of the war; but, I want to stress that this kind of war takes a long time, so that however well-devised the counter-subversion strategy is, its results can only be assessed in the long run.

As long as the people of Mozambique keep their determination, as it happened earlier with the people in Angola in a similar situation; as long as the pace of execution of the project for the resettlement of the population is accelerated and the socio-economic development of the Province continues to be promoted,

I am sure that in a not very distant date Mozambique will know better days.

Q. Has there been a significant shift in Frelimo tactics? If so, why?

A. It can't be said that there has been a significant change in Frelimo tactics, except in what concerns its attitude towards the populations. The enemy continues to avoid direct contact with our armed forces preferring to harass, almost always from a certain distance and under cover of night, our military posts and the troops in operations. However, as far as the populations are concerned, see how Frelimo hounds them, as it happened in Nhacambo, massacring defenceless people, murdering the tribal chiefs and laying mines in the crops, trying to get through terror what it has been unable to get through persuasion.

Q. What role are the Chinese playing in the war?

A. China provides unconditional support to Frelimo, which is no secret to anybody.

That support, a consequence of its policy of penetration in Africa, embraces all kinds of areas: massive supply of material, technical and ideological training of personnel, either in China itself or in Tanzania, diplomatic support, etc.

Q. I believe you have detailed information concerning the definite threat of Frelimo using the Russian "Strella" missile system in the near future. Would you please comment?

A. It is possible that Frelimo comes to use the "Strella" missiles against our planes, if by chance Russia supplies them. We will try to find the adequate antidote, as we did in Guinea; after the initial impact caused by its appearance, we were able to minimise the risks to an acceptable level.

(The "Strella" is a portable ground-to-air missile system. Also known as SAM 7, the "Strella" system caused havoc with American aircraft in Vietnam.)

Q. Would you comment on the military significance of the aldementos (fortified villages)?

A. The military forces are not responsible for the aldeamentos; they are a magnificent effort of socio-economic development for the populations to which the civilian authorities have devoted themselves and the forces under my command give their support, both in their building and improvement and by providing the populations with benefits of an economic, sanitary, religious nature, etc.

Its military importance springs from the fact that, with this scheme, one can ensure a more efficient protection for the populations as well as the benefits of its socio-economic development, as I mentioned before.

Q. Can any assistance be given to the Portuguese war effort by voluntary organisations in South Africa?

A. Given the magnitude and the source of the help Frelimo gets, it would be ridiculous to spurn whatever support can be given to us.

Q. Has the military situation in Mozambique deteriorated?

A. In an overall perspective, we can say that there was an extension of terrorist actions to new areas, which had certain psychological repercussions on a number of the population's sectors, specially the least familiar with the problems of a subversive war.

Q. Could you please comment briefly on the military situations in:
1. Cabo Delgado
2. Niassa
3. Tete
4. Beira/Vila Pery

A. Certainly. It can be said that for the moment the military situation is stabilised in the districts of Niassa and Tete. In Cabo Delgado district an attempt has taken shape to extend subversion beyond the area to which it is confined.

And in the districts of Beira and Vila Pery, the enemy, using very small but very well-trained and aggressive bands, has been able to carry out spectacular actions against targets of non-military nature, namely railway lines, populations still to be settled, etc. It is expected that with the end of the rainy season, in which it is not possible to take full advantage of the available means, with the measures already taken and others which will be soon put into effect, an improvement in this picture of the situation I have, in a general way, drawn for you, will be possible.

This interview was important because it gives a general picture of the military situation in Mozambique just before the military takeover in Portugal. It was also the last interview given by the general.

We left as quickly as we had come, feeling elated as we walked out of the pink two-storey building that is the military headquarters of Mozambique. I was only disappointed I had not got to know the general better. I was not to get the chance as after the coup the general was fired by Portugal's military junta.

That night we celebrated with a bottle of the best Dao wine we could get in Nampula. I learnt that Diogo Neto, the dashing general of the Air Force was still away in Lisbon. At the time I didn't understand the significance of his trip to Portugal, this was only to be clarified on April 25, 1974, when the Government of Portugal fell.

With General Neto away there was no need to be journalists any longer. We had earned our brief respite. I longed to return to the 16th century charm of Mozambique Island, to take a short break from the war and the people involved and transport myself via a two-hour drive back into the past to bask in imagination and feel time disappear.

One of the greatest difficulties of living in the remoter parts of Mozambique is to adjust your concept of time to that of the local residents to many of whom time has no meaning beyond eating, sleeping and drinking. Haste is an unknown quantity in those parts where life is dictated by tides and light and shade, day and night.

But we had work to do, other places to visit, people to see, stories to write. We spent our last night in Nampula away from the war. It was a mental leap – Jimmy with his wife and family back in Johannesburg, me with a burning desire to escape to the island where I could live the life of a dreamer.

The Island had that soporific effect on me. It has a sprititual quality where you really begin to understand why the internal combustion engine was man's greatest invention until somebody turned it on. The island also has many stories surrounding it, some as old as the island itself, some as mysterious as the deep ocean. One concerns a man and the sea – a theme that befits the maritime Portuguese and has fascinated writers since time immemorial.

For the first time in his 56 years, Antonio Duarte Nazareth, a well-known figure in Nampula, decided to go afternoon fishing in the Mozambique Channel. He was a large man, deeply suntanned arms, silver-grey hair flanking an almost young face. He walked with the roll of confidence that some men acquire through a full and generous life. His intimacy was of the back-slapping variety that annoys small men but joins those who are unafraid of their physical nature. He ran a small gun shop in Nampula from where he had arranged his fair share of adventure.

It was one of Antonio's house rules never to brave the ocean in the afternoon because, with darkness around the corner, an accident at sea would mean almost certain death.

On January 19, 1973, he broke his own rule. It was 2 pm and his little wooden fishing boat entered the Mozambique Channel just below the island. With him were two close friends – Catarino, the administrator of a nearby town called Mossuril, who was in his early forties, and Orlando, a 33-year-old scuba diver from Nampula. The three had spent many days together on the ocean, and as the tuna fish were running they looked forward to a short afternoon of good fishing.

The little boat had two outboard motors which brought its prow out of the water as it hydroplaned out to sea against a slight swell. By 3.30 pm the swell had increased and a strong offshore breeze fanned the tops of the waves creating squadrons of white horses and drenching them with salt spray. The engines were difficult to start and after a few hesitant coughs cut out, leaving them to the mercy of the sea. By 4 pm a gale hit the channel and the waves crashed over the frail craft. In that sea the burden of the two engines and the three men was too much and the boat capsized, pitching the three men into the ocean. They clung to the prow which stuck out about a metre above water. A cushion of air caught below water kept it afloat tilted to the storm clouds like the little cork pencil-floats of freshwater anglers.

For hours they clung to the prow as the waves formed mountains of water about them and the gale swept through the troughs whipping the sea into an angry frenzy about them.

As the night took over, Antonio's friends began to weaken: their determination to survive flagged as the waves crashed down, each one like a heavy hammer pounding at them as though obsessed with making them release their grip on the boat's prow. On more than one occasion Antonio slapped their faces and urged them to take courage and hold on. They watched helplessly as in the rare breaks in the storm cloud aircraft scanned the ocean, but the sea was dark, the sky overcast and there was little chance of being seen from the air. Each man was fighting his own battle.

By morning the prow was only 6 centimetres above water and sinking slowly. They still clung on, their fingers locked to the slippery wood and bereft of feeling. It was as though rigor mortis had locked their fingers forever. Antonio thought it better to leave the boat. He realised that when it sank they would be sucked under with it. He dived under water and wrenched one of the benches out of the boat.

"I must leave now," he said to his friends. "The boat will sink any moment. If you stay with it you will die."

Catarino, the administrator, couldn't swim and was too tired to leave, so grasping the water-logged bench, Antonio and Orlando, a good swimmer, said goodbye and drifted slowly away in the swell. It was a sad parting, but one in which there were courage and affection, a last quiet farewell – no dramatics between three men looking death in the face.

Antonio and Orlando had drifted 30 metres away when Orlando changed his mind. He decided to go back to the boat. He let go of the bench and began swimming back. He was too weak, and Antonio saw him slip beneath the surface without protest as though glad to end the awful struggle. A little later Catarino joined Orlando as the boat sank.

Through the long hours of the day, Antonio clung to his bench, bobbing on the ocean until 22 hours later he was sighted by a crew member of a Dutch cargo vessel, the *Straat Le Maire*. He was picked out of the ocean 30 kilometres from Mozambique Island.

The crew helped Antonio aboard and he fell into a deep sleep in the warm comfort of a bunk. His eyes and face were swollen and chaffed from the salt water and the wind. Later in the day he was wakened by the captain, who told him he would be put ashore in Dar es Salaam, in Tanzania.

Antonio was still weak, but full of spirit, and in a weary voice he said to the captain: "You would have done better to leave me in the ocean. I am Portuguese; if you put me ashore in Tanzania, I will rot the rest of my life away in a prison cell." The captain didn't argue because a Portuguese naval destroyer that had picked up the Dutch boat's message about Antonio persuaded him courteously to head for Porto Amelia rather than Dar es Salaam.

Antonio Duarte Nazareth's ordeal with the ocean was over. He had lost 14 kilograms in weight and had lost his two closest friends. From that day on he has never put his foot in a boat again. "I respect the dead," was how he put it.

He told me sometime later that the Portuguese spirit can never be crushed. "But there is one thing I do know, although it can survive the ocean, it cannot survive in Africa."

I was not to see Nampula again for nearly two months when I returned reluctantly to report on developments in Mozambique after the military takeover in Portugal.

CHAPTER SEVEN

CABORA BASSA: TETE AND SONGO

The district of Tete, which is cut off from the main body of Mozambique by Malawi to the east and bordered by Zambia to the north, is where the Portuguese made their greatest contribution to the territory with the building of the giant Cabora Bassa Hydro-electric scheme. But it was also in Tete that the Portuguese made a fatal military miscalculation.

Whereas, from the beginning of hostilities in the north, the Portuguese had been building aldeamentos, or fortified villages, to bring the widespread population together for protection and control, nothing similar had been done in the Tete district.

In the north the aldeamentos provided a number of services to the inhabitants. Health services; social and educational facilities were provided that had gone a long way to improve the Portuguese image among the residents. In the north the Portuguese also had the support of the Mucua tribe, the largest of Mozambique's tribal groups with about 2-million members. The Mucuas are also the traditional enemies of the Maconde people from whom Frelimo got most of its support and recruits in the north.

In the Tete district, the Portuguese had not built aldeamentos and nor could they rely on the support of the local population.

The first reports of attacks in the Tete district date back to 1968, when small groups of guerrillas attacked the communications systems in and around the Cabora Bassa hydro-electric scheme, which is being built near Songo, about 100 kilometres from the town of Tete itself. But the major guerrilla thrust into the Tete district came after 1970 when the Portuguese military high command decided to try a counter offensive against Frelimo in Cabo Delgado, in the north of Mozambique.

It was the largest offensive in the history of the war. "Gordion Knot", as it was called, was the brainchild of the former Commander-in-chief, General Kaulza De Arriaga.

De Arriaga believed he could wipe Frelimo out in the north once and for all and he nearly did. But instead of standing and fighting, the Frelimo forces melted back into the bush and went across the

Rovuma River into Tanzania. Frelimo then decided to concentrate more on infiltration into the Tete district and let the Portuguese offensive in Cabo Delgado peter out. Using Zambia and later Malawi as stepping-off points into the Tete district, the Frelimo groups got a firm foothold in the district and a third area had been opened for guerrilla operations. In an interesting paper on Portugal's wars in Africa, Neil Bruce, writing for *Conflict Studies* in London gives three reasons for the neglect of the Tete district:

1. "The army, with its headquarters at Nampula in the north, was naturally chiefly concerned with the Frelimo threat southwards from Tanzania, and south-eastwards down the edge of Lake Malawi – and it seemed, after the big 1970 military operation, largely to have succeeded in containing this movement and stopping the southward pressure.

2. "There seemed to be no obvious threat to Tete, from within or without, except for the occasional laying of mines by Coremo (another Guerrilla movement operating out of Zambia), which was easily dealt with by the small army garrisons. To the south was the friendly country of Rhodesia; and to the east the equally friendly country of Malawi. Road traffic ran freely between Rhodesia and Malawi; and the frontier with Zambia was quiet and virtually deserted. There seemed no reason to expect an organised move by Frelimo 700 miles away when they seemed already fully committed.

3. "Tete district and its inhabitants were peaceful. All energies were devoted to work on the giant Cabora Bassa Dam, planning the move of populations from the area to be flooded by the vast lake to be formed, and the provision of training in new agricultural techniques and services for the new villages and settlements to be created. Traffic had been quite normal on the road and rail from the coast to the site of Cabora Bassa.

"The over-confidence and the lack of preparation – especially social – among the tribes on the borders of Tete, nevertheless seem remarkable at first sight; especially in view of the emphasis placed on social developments, on winning the hearts and minds of the people in other places. But Nampula was far away from Tete, and so was the Governor-General's office in Lourenco

Marques, chiefly concerned with bringing the infrastructure of the Province up to date as quickly as possible. This was a difficult job, given the inadequate statistics available, and the extent to which the real poverty of the country was disguised by a construction boom and influx of luxury consumer goods into the city shops. This was also true in Beira – and the ever-increasing flood of tourists there and elsewhere, which did not suggest a dangerous situation in Tete or the centre and south".

But a dangerous situation did exist and one that was worsening by the day as the Frelimo groups operating in the district systematically subverted or terrorised the locals to their cause and disrupted Portuguese communication systems, notably those serving the Cabora Bassa Dam.

It was with this backdrop that we arrived in Tete which is one of the hottest spots in Southern Africa. By noon a haze of reflected heat rises off the streets giving the town a distorted look. Tete is hard to the bank of the Zambesi River about 500 kilometres from where it flows into the Indian Ocean.

The town was founded as a Portuguese trading post in 1531 and as the years rolled by it experienced its fair share of drama. It was at Tete that Dr David Livingstone, the British missionary-explorer halted during his walk across the continent from the Atlantic to the Indian Ocean.

Like many of the frontier towns in Africa, Tete has an undefined atmosphere of earthiness about it as if just below the surface all the history of Portugal in Africa is straining to emerge and unfold itself.

Tete has become one of the most throbbing towns in Mozambique. The planning and organisation of the Cabora Bassa Dam actually began in 1957, before the war had even started, and once building operations began, the town developed fast until today it is the most go-ahead town in Mozambique.

The main purpose of our visit was to fly on to Songo, about 100 kilometres to the west, where the Cabora Bassa Dam is being constructed. While we were there, however, I heard that Zeca Caliante, a former Frelimo commander who defected to the Portuguese, was working there.

Caliante had been one of the four Frelimo commanders in the Tete district before his defection in July, 1973. He had been a militant member of Frelimo for nine years, trained in Nachingwea, Frelimo's principle base in Tanzania, and was a key man in the Frelimo set-up in Mozambique. His defection was important to the Portuguese, for although Frelimo propaganda played down his significance, Caliante had a lot to tell about Frelimo and wasn't adverse to telling it to the Portuguese.

He had been recruited to Frelimo in 1962 when he was offered a scholarship to study outside Mozambique. He accepted and found himself at Nachingwea studying the gentle art of guerrilla warfare. He was then sent to the Tete district as an adviser and later was promoted to commander of one of the four Frelimo sections operating in Tete.

After his defection, Caliante worked for the Portuguese army's department of propaganda (APSIC). His job was to drop propaganda leaflets on the local populations in Tete and broadcast propaganda messages from a specially converted light aircraft.

I met him on a hot afternoon. He was preparing the plane with the pilot for a pamphlet drop later in the day, and although my talk with him was brief it was important. Zeca Caliante was not a very endearing personality. He wore sunglasses and looked intense as if he resented being questioned on his past. Well built, medium height and prone to wear flashy clothes, Caliante had probably seen so many inquisitive people since his defection that he wished he had stayed in the bush. He had an almost surly disposition.

His first claim was significant. He said that Chinese instructers were supporting the guerrilla movement from Tanzania and that they had begun to take an active part in the war in Cabo Delgado. He claimed they were now directing operations against troops and civilians in the north.

He also claimed there were no Frelimo base camps in Malawi, which is hostile to the guerrilla movements, but that Frelimo troops moved freely through Malawian territory on their way south. (For the list of guerrilla base camps and their purposes see appendix two.)

Caliante also made the point that there was no direct radio communication between individual Frelimo groups in Mozambique. Contact is maintained through headquarters in Dar es Salaam, in Tanzania.

Caliante was also outspoken in his condemnation of the present president of Frelimo, Samora Machel, whom is called: "An ambitious criminal" and that the entire organisation of Frelimo was infiltrated by Chinese. "I can assure you Frelimo is entirely infiltrated by Red Chinese," he said.

I got Caliante to draw me a diagram of the organisation of the defence department of Frelimo, which I found tallied fairly closely with the official organisational structure I had in my possession. (See appendix one.)

Zeca Caliante's claims were similar to those of another important Frelimo defector, Alves Muganga, who had been responsible for Frelimo recruitment and was even more senior in the Frelimo ranks than Caliante.

Muganga disclosed squabbling in the ranks of Frelimo. He called the president, Samora Machel: "A Mao Tse-tung puppet and a tool in the hands of Moscow. He is tyrannical and lacks intelligence," said Muganga. He told Pressmen that although Russia was still supplying arms and training men in their use, the Chinese were in firm control of Frelimo.

"Violence against the civilian population will not stop while the Chinese give orders to Frelimo," said Muganga. He claimed that Samora Machel's dictatorship was brutal and that Frelimo atrocities were committed on instruction from the Chinese. "I can swear that Mozambique would be converted into a bloody field of tribal rivalries if Frelimo wins this war," he said. He also claimed that until 1969, 154 Frelimo men were given scholarships and of these only two returned to Frelimo. The others decided to stay in the countries in which they studied: in Eastern Europe, Canada and America.

The accuracy of these claims is impossible to judge. Portuguese intelligence and informed sources close to the military told me that a group of 30 Chinese had been operating in Cabo Delgado, advising Frelimo groups on how to conduct their guerrilla operations. There had been unconfirmed reports of Chinese being captured in the north, but I could not find any concrete evidence of this, and because of the diplomatically explosive nature of the issue, my questions on the subject were always circumvented.

But that the Chinese were heavily involved in the war in the north I have little doubt. Soldiers have shown me Mao's little red book taken from dead Frelimos and on one occasion I was shown a blood-stained plastic wallet with Chinese markings by a volunteer soldier in the north.

But the Chinese influence is not basically military. China provides most of the small arms and although military instructors teach Frelimo recruits the subtleties of guerrilla warfare in base camps in Tanzania, the Chinese main contribution to Frelimo is in what the Portuguese call "mentalisation". The Portuguese claim it takes them two years to rehabilitate mentally a man who has been in the hands of a Chinese psychological instructor for only six months. Chinese methods of press-gang ideological instruction far outstripped the Portuguese, who had to rely on the secret police, DGS, to try to unscramble mentally captured Frelimos' minds. It was a hopeless task.

It would seem then that Chinese tactics in the war in Mozambique have been to convert Frelimo from a bona fide Black Nationalist movement to a "vanguard of the proletariat", to use Frelimo to instill a revolutionary fervour in the people of Mozambique who would then rise up and throw the "colonial oppressors" out, remembering always who gave them the means to do it.

The Chinese influence made it obvious that the nature of the war in Mozambique was psychological not military and Portuguese counter-propaganda was not sophisticated enough to match the Chinese. I learnt that the Chinese had established a powerful radio transmitter in Dar es Salaam which beamed Maoist and Frelimo propaganda to Mozambique where Frelimo political agents had distributed large numbers of fixed-station transistor radios. Communication experts largely agree that radio is the most powerful propaganda vehicle among the various media available.

This was one of the reasons a Russian submarine was beaming anti-Chinese radio propaganda into Tanzania and northern Mozambique, to try to counteract Chinese propaganda in that sphere. The presence of Soviet submarine transmitters off the Mozambique coast gives strength to the claims that China is now pulling the strings in Tanzania, and Russia's Red star is waning.

In the sophisticated battle for semi-illiterate and illiterate minds in Mozambique, it makes one wonder what chance the average villager has.

What does a tribesman know about NATO, the UN or the OAU let alone the origin of the messages that are battering his mind for all these diverse sources?

Finnish students had also donated a printing press to Frelimo which prints Frelimo propaganda leaflets in Dar es Salaam, which are in turn distributed in Mozambique.

Portuguese counter-propaganda is largely unsophisticated. They tack billboards around villages in the bush urging the population to move into the fortified villages and spread the message of violence and poverty that would accompany liaison with Frelimo. They drop pamphlets and broadcast from the air. Before the coup in Portugal, all the media in Mozambique were censored and cinema news-reels were embarrassing in their propaganda content.

The war was actually the catalyst for Portuguese attempts to uplift the local population. I think the Portuguese would agree with this statement. They laid great stress on the efforts they were making to educate, house and provide health services for the local populations. But Frelimo propaganda could always keep ahead by promising more without having to fulfill the promises. As the war progressed, it became obvious that Frelimo was keeping ahead in the propaganda race and this realisation was one of the reasons for the military takeover in Portugal.

The sophistication of Chinese influence in the war in Mozambique can be judged by the continuance of COREMO (Comité Revolucionário de Moçambique – Revolutionary Committee for Mozambique), a guerrilla organisation based in Zambia.

Coremo is Maoist-orientated and is heavily influenced by the Chinese. Although Frelimo is the most highly organised and motivated guerrilla organisation in Southern Africa, Coremo still operates freely in Mozambique, often with considerable opposition from Frelimo.

The Chinese used Coremo as a backstop in case their influence in Frelimo should cease. If Frelimo had rid itself of the Chinese influence, the Chinese would have switched their full support to Coremo, which could continue to further Chinese motives in Southern Africa.

Since the coup, Coremo made it known that it would be prepared to enter Mozambique and establish itself as a legitimate political party to fight in open elections.

Caliante was quite outspoken in his condemnation of the Chinese and his outspokenness was part of the Portuguese propaganda campaign. The Portuguese propaganda leaflets often picture defectors who tell the local people not to support Frelimo. Although Caliante told me his propaganda campaign was having a measure of success, there was little doubt in my mind that Frelimo was winning grass-root support at an alarming rate.

Another interesting disclosure came from this meeting with Caliante. The pilot of his aircraft was none other than Jose Santos, better known to thousands of South African soccer enthusiasts as "Santos", the former Southern Suburbs goalkeeper. Jose had switched his prowess at saving goals to saving souls. As a commercial pilot he had been contracted by the Portuguese army to fly propaganda missions and he and Caliante were flying twice a day throughout the Tete district.

The evening before we flew from Tete to Songo to visit the Cabora Bassa Dam, we were sitting in the dining-room of the Hotel Zambesi, which has one of the best tables in Mozambique, when we heard a commotion in the street below. I left the table and took the old gilt lift downstairs.

As I walked into the cool evening, three lorry loads of dishevelled Portuguese commandos drove around the corner in front of the hotel. They were brandishing banners and singing. From their appearance they had been in the bush a long time. Nobody took much notice, but in the back of one of the trucks I noticed two men in a slightly different colour camouflage. They were tied together and two Black commandos were covering them with captured Kalashnikovs, Chinese-built assault rifles used by many of the guerrillas. As the trucks disappeared down the dirt road, the dust following them like a sullen brown cloud, I couldn't help thinking it strange that Zeca Caliante, now working for the Portuguese army, could well have been one of those captured guerrillas going to a fate unknown instead of being a key figure in the Portuguese propaganda programme. Such is the nature of this war.

The flight to Songo was a bit hair raising. The town is often covered with a low cloud base and on the morning we flew out, we had waited for two hours at the airport for it to lift. It looked as though the pilot had overslept, and when I saw his wife I could understand why.

Songo nestles in a range of hills and the aircraft flew between them, heading for one peak then breaking away down a valley before heading for another. It was like flying through the corridors of the mind avoiding each new emotional mountain that loomed up before

95

me. Below, the Zambesi meandered lazily around the hills, building up momentum as it passed through each new gorge until it finally tumbled with its full force through the most contentious gorge on the African continent – Cabora Bassa.

Cabora Bassa, the Portuguese "crime against humanity", to quote President Kaunda of Zambia, is the cornerstone of Portuguese development planning in Mozambique. For the Portuguese it represents the spark that could ignite a new life for millions of people in Mozambique, develop the Zambesi Valley and provide the power to exploit the vast potential mineral wealth of the territory.

The local tribesmen found the great gorge where the dam is being built an inaccessible obstacle for their frail canoes and gave it the name Cabora Bassa – "Where the work ends". It was at Cabora Bassa that they lifted their canoes from the Zambesi and rested their weary bodies.

But for the Portuguese it was where the work began – the generation of the spark that, they claim, is to set Mozambique on the road to exploiting its potential wealth, make it economically viable and procure a place in the sun for the country's 8,5-million people.

A visit to Cabora Bassa is a study in contrasts. Songo has built up around the project, a flat lustreless little construction camp in the heart of the Zambesi Valley where the giant project is directed and co-ordinated. Songo houses about 14 000 people – an odd mixture of cultures, languages and national interests, but all intent on one thing: to build the dam and assert man's dominance in concrete over Nature.

In Songo it is not unusual to find small groups of people speaking French or Italian, English or Portuguese. It is one of those strange cosmopolitan phenomena that spring up in the African bush wherever a large development is underway and is supported by Western countries.

It is not an ordinary civil engineering project. To the 5 000 people actually working on the dam site, it is a vast challenge slowly but surely being overcome as the great concrete slopes inch their way higher to mock the boiling Zambesi below.

Songo is really a small slice of Europe slap in the middle of the steaming African bush. Its little "international" airport is like a miniature Heathrow as visitors, officials, engineers and workmen from many different nations fly in and out with their passports at

Portugal's gentle revolution . . . Portuguese rebel troops drive through the streets of Lisbon.—Picture: Courtesy United Press International.

Frelimo supporters disrupt a political meeting organised by GUMO in Lourenco Marques, capital of Mozambique, soon after the military takeover in Portugal.
—Picture: Mike McCann.

the ready. Even a Russian journalist has passed through Immigration at Songo's airport.

His name was Victor Louis and was believed to have close ties with the Kremlin's KGB secret police.

Louis obtained permission to visit Mozambique during a visit to Lisbon in December 1973. His arrival in Mozambique in February caused considerable speculation in the territory. He was there for two weeks and visited the war areas in the north and the military headquarters in Nampula.

As with all of Mozambique, before the coup in Portugal, immigration was handled by DGS, the secret police, and security was tight. It reminded me of a visit I made to the Pentagon in Washington, as the DGS official inspected our papers with an inscrutable face. A group of Rhodesian tourists arrived with us without prior permission to visit Songo let alone Cabora Bassa.

"You can't come in," said the official.

The pilot was a Rhodesian "colonial" character. His red face bristled with indignation and he exploded into a frenzy, dropping names of people he knew in Tete and even in Songo in an attempt to get his party through. They stood behind him with their shooting sticks and cameras with a type of benign disinterest and an obvious distaste for the treatment they were receiving. The pilot eventually persuaded the official that he and his party were only sightseers and were only staying for the morning.

"Dashed curse all this red tape nonsense," said the pilot to his party. They agreed.

At the airport we were met by Alcidio De Carvalho, public relations officer for the Zambesi Plan Bureau (GPZ) in Songo. GPZ is the official Portuguese body responsible for the development of the Zambesi Valley.

Alcidio was more French than Portuguese and his English had a distinct French accent. I thought at the time his Portuguese must have been a treat to the ear. He was tall and casual like a successful executive on leave. He refused to get excited either about our arrival or the rantings of our Rhodesian friends who were still smarting in the airport lounge at the treatment they had received.

"How long will you be staying?" Alcidio asked.

"As long as it takes us to see the project and get the pictures we need."

97

Alcidio thought for a moment then said: "Where will you be staying?"

"In the hotel," I answered naively.

"There's no hotel in Songo."

"How about on the airport terminal?"

"I don't think that will be possible."

"Well, in that case, we will sleep under the stars."

"Yes, you won't be the first to have done that," said Alcidio.

"Have you any better suggestions?" I asked.

"You could try the country club. They have a few rooms. Perhaps one is vacant."

Alcidio was a bit too casual for my liking.

As I expected, there was a vacant room at the club. Later that morning we discussed our programme with Alcidio.

"I can't take you to the site this morning; I must take the Rhodesians because they leave this afternoon," he said.

"Fine, but if that's the case how about us hi-jacking the GPZ helicopter and flying over the site this morning to take some photographs."

"I don't think that will be possible. The helicopter has a set schedule, but I will try."

An hour later we were suspended over the dam wall, the verdant hills surrounding the dam towering above the hovering aircraft. Neither we nor Alcidio seemed to worry about what had happened to the Rhodesian party.

At first sight the dam wall was an anti-climax. I had expected something quite breathtaking, something to match my imagination. The workmen had already completed one side that appeared to cling precariously to the right bank as if it was about to fall back and get swallowed by the turbulence below. It all seemed incomplete, great blocks of concrete rising out of the river, without pattern, without form.

I nudged Jimmy Soullier sitting next to me in the back. "What do you think?" "Not much," he said. "Alcidio has got the pilot to hover so that I can hardly see the dam. I'm a short guy, don't forget."

Alcidio was up front with the pilot snapping off the odd picture with his Instamatic through the cockpit perspex. In the back Jimmy was fuming, thousands of rands worth of sophisticated camera equipment lying useless on the seat as Alcidio, with self-concern, snapped his shutter lens. Soon we were whizzing back to Songo.

"Good pictures?" asked Alcidio.

"Great, really great," said Jimmy. "I'll send you a postcard."

It is only when you approach the dam wall from the ground that you realise the size of the project. When complete, the top of the dam wall will curve 300 metres from bank to bank and rise 170 metres into the air – enough concrete to hold back the Zambesi in a dam that will stretch over 250 kilometres back into the interior toward the Zambian border.

While the dam wall was being completed, the river was diverted through two underground tunnels through the hills on either side of the gorge to emerge on the other side of the dam wall. The tunnels were due to be closed off in October and the water behind the wall would start rising immediately and with it the Portuguese hope for a better economic future in Mozambique.

In March, 1975, the first power from the dam is scheduled to hum through the 1 380 kilometres of transmission lines to the Apollo Power Station, near Pretoria, in South Africa, as the first three turbines at the dam go into operation.

There are five turbines in all that will collectively generate 2 000 mw of electricity, making Cabora Bassa Africa's largest hydro-electric power source and the fourth largest in the world. The two largest dams in Portugal produce less than one turbine at Cabora Bassa.

When I visited it, the dam was well on schedule despite the avowed promises from Frelimo that if the guerrillas could not destroy it, they would make it far more costly and delay its construction. The transmission lines to South Africa were already completed — six months ahead of schedule.

Here the facts end and the speculation begins. Basically, Cabora Bassa means many things to many people. It is a symbol and a focal point of contention in Africa. To the Portuguese, the dam underscored their repeated denials that Portugal would pull out of Mozambique even if their position in the territory deteriorated, and the R100 000 a day Portugal was paying ZAMCO, the international consortium that is building the dam, was a strong reinforcement of that denial.

The Portuguese saw the project as the beginning of a new Mozambique, one that would turn the scales against their enemies and fly in the eye of a hostile world intent on discrediting Portuguese motives in her overseas province of Mozambique. As the charter accepting ZAMCO's tender for the project stated: " . . . the Cabora Bassa undertaking will be a landmark to exemplify and consolidate Portuguese policy in the provinces in Africa."

But that was before the Government of Portugal was ousted by the Movement of the Armed Forces on April 25, 1974. Since that day a huge question mark hangs over the entire project. It would seem hard to believe that Portugal built the dam only to hand over to Frelimo. The coup in Portugal brought with it the nagging doubt about the future of Mozambique and the possibility of rapid independence and the possible severing of ties with metropolitan Portugal as a result. There was also the possibility of a unilateral declaration of independence in Mozambique, much like Rhodesia's UDI. The question was: where did Cabora Bassa come into the scheme of things after the coup?

Portuguese thinking on Mozambique since the coup was that Mozambique would move gradually toward self-determination under the guiding wing of Mother Portugal. Portugal hoped Mozambique would make a choice about its future that would keep the territory in a loose association with metropolitan Portugal. That way everyone would benefit from the development that would flow from the Cabora Bassa scheme.

It is an optimistic ideal and the question mark still remains about the project: not that it will be completed, for it will, but who will eventually reap the benefits?

To Frelimo, the guerrilla movement bent on throwing the Portuguese out of Mozambique, the project had a very different meaning. In 1968, Dr Eduardo Mondlane, the former president of Frelimo before his assassination in Dar es Salaam, said, "If we do not destroy the Caborra Bassa Dam scheme, or at least make it twice as costly, we will have received our greatest setback."

But the success of the Frelimo war effort dictated a different approach to the entire scheme. Far from suffering a setback through the construction of the dam, Frelimo may have had an inkling of the future. Frelimo knew as well as the Portuguese that the war in Mozambique could only have a political solution. With this knowledge it would have been self-defeating to try to destroy the project and, in any case, Frelimo didn't have the military capability to destroy it or even significantly to hold up its construction.

This view is supported by the fact that only token resistance was put up by Frelimo to the construction of the dam. The cement convoy bringing materials from Tete to Songo twice a day was regularly attacked or the road mined, but Frelimo never attempted to strike at the dam site.

At any stage after the transmission lines were built, Frelimo groups could have sabotaged pylons, but at the time of writing this had not been attempted although Frelimo groups had used the transmission lines as a natural compass for their sojourns through the Tete district.

It seems likely, then that Frelimo decided not to strike at Cabora Bassa except through a few token gestures of defiance, just to let the Portuguese know that they were still around.

But initial hostility to the project came not only from Frelimo. President Kaunda of Zambia called it "a crime against humanity" and the General Assembly of the United Nations voted overwhelmingly for a motion calling on governments of member countries to prevent their citizens and corporations under their control from participating in the scheme.

"The project is intended to entrench colonialist and racist domination over the territories in Africa and is a source of international tension," was how the Assembly worded it.

But member countries of the United Nations did participate in the R500-million project. Besides the Portuguese, France, Italy, West Germany and South Africa have a stake in the form of a long-term loan of 50 per cent of the cost of the dam. It is significant that after the coup, the South African Parliament did not cut off finance for the scheme. Instead it cut back the 1974 appropriation, adopting a "wait-and-see" attitude.

On the site itself nobody seems particularly concerned about the politics of the whole thing or the possibility of Frelimo attacking the dam.

"There is no threat," said Braz De Oliveira, the director of the project in Songo. He was a short, balding man with a busy air about him that made me keep the interview short. He seemed ready to answer any question with confidence as if he had answered them all before long ago – to himself.

"This is my sixth dam and my last before retiring and, yes, of

101

course, it will be intact when I retire. Indeed, it is big enough to despense with words." Big enough to dispense with words, yes, but not with precautions. Security for the dam is the responsibility of ZOT, the Zone of Tete military command in Tete, about 100 kilometres away. Questions about security were treated with care, but the army is known to have built a tight cordon around the dam site and it is said to be surrounded by the largest mine-field in the world. Dogs were also used in the defence of Cabora Bassa and the cavalry are expected to operate in the area.

But all these things were of little interest to the men on site and like the local tribesmen many years before them who looked forward to reaching Cabora Bassa where the work would end, they, too, await the day when their part in the gigantic task will be done.

We were sitting talking to Ernie Christie, one of Africa's top cine cameramen, in the clubhouse. Ernie is the very picture of success, topping the bill as a matured raconteur and man of action. It was Ernie who covered the Congo crisis and the war in Vietnam, which established his reputation as top of the tree in his profession. He was down in Songo filming the progress of the dam for LTA, a South African construction company that was building all the underground installations for the dam.

Ernie had flown into Songo in his light aircraft to take some more film and as we sat on the stoep discussing the war, he seemed to crystalise the whole concept of Cabora Bassa in a few pithy sentences. "Why not let the Portuguese build it for them?" He was talking about Frelimo. "That is exactly what the Vietcong did in Vietnam. Let the Americans get on with all the development while they sat back."

He also related an incident from the story book he has accumulated during his four-year filming involvement with the Cabora Bassa scheme. Four years ago, according to Ernie, there was only one taxi in the town of Tete. He had some urgent business in Malawi and rather than wait for the next flight out decided to take the taxi. So off they went to Zomba, in Malawi, a good 250 kilometres away. The taxi driver couldn't believe his good fortune, and, said Ernie with a wink, gave up his taxi business and bought a farm with the fare, where he has built up a highly lucrative market-gardening business.

Another character worth mentioning in the Tete district is Evaristo

Fernandes, the CIT (Government tourist agency) representative in Tete. Evaristo was one of the only Portuguese officials I met in Mozambique who understood the concept of time. He had a peculiar habit of arriving a few minutes early for arrangements, which threw us right out as we banked on at least 20 minutes before each appointment would materialise.

Evaristo had an aching need for sheet music to continue the music lessons he gave to the neighbourhood children. He told me that John Osman, the BBC correspondent in Southern Africa, based in Johannesburg, had promised to send some sheet music for him, or to arrange with a Johannesburg company to have it sent on a monthly basis, but he had heard nothing. I promised to do likewise, but found in Johannesburg that no company I approached was interested because they didn't want to be paid in escudos.

It was months later that I saw John Osman in Lourenco Marques and mentioned Evaristo's problem to him. But I need not have worried. John had made arrangements in Johannesburg, and I have no doubt Evaristo is now swamped with sheet music and that Tete is ringing to the sounds of Evaristo's pupils' dexterous fingers running up and down the keyboards.

CHAPTER EIGHT

A CHRONICLE OF MISERY: THE HOSPITALS

One of my assignments as a reporter in Mozambique, was to see what toll the war was taking in human resources. It meant on every possible occasion going through the military hospitals; speaking to the injured, Portuguese soldiers and Frelimo guerrillas; looking critically at the hospital conditions and, in that way, trying to assess the intensity of the war. It was not a pleasant task and one that I did through necessity and not through any personal desire.

The military hospital at Tete was the second of two major field hospitals I visited. We were taken around the hospital by an extremely disinterested young Portuguese officer, which only added to the depression of the place. Outside the hospital's military section, as with all the field hospitals, was the helicopter pad. Injured were flown in from the bush by helicopters directly to the hospital, or if the injury was not too serious, evacuated from the bush, patched up in a base camp and them flown to Tete in a light aircraft. From the airfield he would then be rushed to the hospital in an ambulance.

We arrived about 10 a.m. and sat near the helipad in case an injured soldier was brought in. It was hot; the white glare from the hospital buildings reflected back, lighting the area like a Hollywood studio set.

Occasionally medical orderlies would pass by, some with plastic packets of plasma, other clutching bottles as the edges of their linen housecoats caught in the breeze or flapped around their knees. There was a certain organised haste about these men, totally different from the soldiers who lounged around, smoking, chatting or leaning against walls dreaming.

At 10,45 we heard the helicopter in the distance chopping through the air as it came in over the Zambesi, hugging the outside bank before turning at right angles and coming straight for the hospital.

With the sound of the aircraft, a door to one of the wards opened and eight orderlies came out and walked briskly to the helipad. Beside it were two stretchers - one still bloodstained - which stand next to the pad 24 hours a day.

The helicopter landed, the door opened and an unconscious figure was put on to one of the stretchers. The helicopter left as quickly as it had arrived, spinning off on the same tack it had come in on and heading out over the Zambesi River.

They carried the man carefully off the helipad and toward the open ward. As they passed me, I looked at him. He was young, very young, and a little later I learned that he had been blown up by a mine. His eyes were swollen and water oozed out of them like glycerine tears – the result of sand that had been thrown up into his face with the explosion of the mine.

His dark face was contorted, pinched in pain and his tongue lolled about in a dry mouth. His right arm dangled off the side of the stretcher, and three of the fingers were missing, leaving a pulpy wound that had once been the man's hand. I wondered whether those hands had ever created anything of beauty and if they had whether they ever would again, had they ever fondled a woman in love? Had they ever reached to the sky, touched the earth or covered his eyes in time of torment?

His camouflage suit had been ripped apart below the waist, completely torn from the right leg and peppered with small holes up to the waist. His right leg was off below the knee, the mutilation, grisly.

It was all over in a matter of seconds. He had disappeared into the hospital, to an emergency operating theatre, where the wounds would be cleaned and patched up so that in time he could emerge alive, but without the use of two of his limbs. In time that would heal as well, it always does, but who can tell how deep the mental wounds would be, how heavy this man's cross would be.

An hour later the helicopter returned and another young man, this time Black, was hauled out of the back seat like a carcass and carried off to a surgeon's scalpel in the theatre. It seemed such a waste, so degrading to see men mutilated – some dying – being carried off in this manner and such a waste that the surgeons' skills should have to go to patching broken bodies that only hours before were upright and healthy. The effect is to create a vision of man as ultimately bestial, ultimately vile and putrescent: without dignity: ugly and unworthy – and man is none of these.

Later in the day a dead soldier was brought in. We had met a volunteer South African nurse from Durban. She told us it was the fifth death from cholera in the Tete district that week. Nobody had warned us about the outbreak of cholera in the area. We both went straight off and had a booster cholera shot.

Tete Hospital is remarkable for the number of mine victims who fill its beds. Most of them are not soldiers, but civilians who have trodden on mines or tracks leading to and from their villages or in nearby fields where the locals grow a few crops. Up to December, 1973, 700 villagers – men, women and children – had been killed by mines and nearly 2 000 had been maimed for life. One of them was a nine-year-old boy named Faustino.

Faustino's story is not all that different from any number of young boys and girls who have had their limbs ripped off by mines in the Tete district. He had been on an errand for his mother, left the village and walked down a track leading to the river. Minutes later he was lying beside the track both his legs torn off, at a place called Chifisse – the "Place of Disaster". I saw Faustino months after, propped up in his wheelchair, terribly shy, but smiling up at me as I talked to one of the Black nurses who attended to him and the hundreds like him who have been treated at Tete hospital. Faustino was still too young to understand what the loss of his legs meant to his life. I wondered whether realisation would turn into bitterness or understanding – the former seemed more likely.

I wrote about Faustino in an article in the Johannesburg *Sunday Times* three weeks later and received a letter from a woman in the Transvaal enclosing some money to be sent to the boy. Journalism has its rewards.

While I was in Nampula, the military headquarters of Mozambique, I had visited the military hospital there. The hospital is on the outskirts of the town and it is not an uncommon sight to see an ambulance rushing through the town taking another victim from the airport to the hospital. Having seen the inside of that hospital and drawn impressions of the staff and men there, I would try to imagine the men inside those ambulances, what they looked like before and what they would look like after. The tragedy of it is that you rarely see them before only afterwards; some you never see at all.

Nampula Military Hospital serves the entire north of Cabo Delgado. It is businesslike and always full of patients. I visited it twice. My first visit was to meet the director of the hospital, Dr Bastos. The doctor met us outside and took us back into his little office in the administrative wing. It was more like a wall-to-wall filing cabinet. In those files were kept all the statistics about injuries and the injured, the sad statistical story of 10 years of war in the north.

The doctor was fidgety, always moving about and he made no attempt to hide his dislike for us. He was evasive on statistical questions and, as we went through some of the files, he was reluctant to explain the full statistical picture. He claimed 50 per cent of the patients were suffering from tropical diseases, 25 per cent were accident victims and the balance were seriously injured in combat. It is difficult to get an accurate picture. Official figures released for the last three months of 1973 showed 74 deaths from sickness and 58 killed in action.

Dr Bastos was a dentist by training, but at Nampula Hospital he was doing surgical operations. This seemed understandable because of the shortage of surgeons. Nampula Hospital had only two surgical teams and one of the surgeons was an optometrist. The hospital has 400 beds, which are usually filled and when I visited it there were 20 doctors.

A visit through the wards gives a depressing glimpse into the nature of this cruel war – in which most of the seriously wounded have lost limbs through mine blasts. Portuguese troops rarely make contact with Frelimo groups in the bush and the guerrillas avoid contact as far as possible. Instead, they concentrate on disrupting communications and laying mines in the path of oncoming troops or convoys. They are past-masters in the grim business of mine warfare – a fact borne out by the number of mine casualties in the hospitals.

Combat injured are treated in field hospitals like Nampula until the chances of infection are minimised. More serious casualties are flown direct to the University Hospital in the capital, Lourenco Marques. Amputees, who constitute the vast majority of these, are psychologically rehabilitated in Lourenco Marques by trained psychiatrists. Some, the more fortunate, are then flown to West Germany to be fitted with artificial limbs to begin their new and very much restricted lives.

I was interested to know about compensation for the serious victims of the war. I was told that amputees are given a small transistor radio and 200 escudos (about R5) a month compensation for their disability. Their injuries seem a high price to pay for this steady income.

During one of my visits to the hospital the floor of one of the wards was awash with dirty water. In the ward were men whose wounds could easily have become infected, but nobody seemed to be overly concerned about the condition of the ward. It was there that I met a 27-year-old Maconde tribesman, who called himself Pereira. There was something about the man that made me stop and enter the room. There were only two beds, one unoccupied beneath a window and the other pushed up against the inside wall. I stood at the end of Pereira's bed leaning against the wall, watching. It was a sight I will never forget.

Pereira wasn't a soldier. He had been recruited by a company of Portuguese commandos as their guide during an operation against a Frelimo band in Cabo Delgado. He had followed the guerrillas' tracks through the thick bush until the previous day when he had stepped on an anti-personnel mine in a clearing. The explosion had blown up into his groin and mutilated his foot beyond recognition. He had been evacuated from the bush by helicopter to Nampula Hospital where his left leg had been amputated below the knee. He had regained consciousness a few hours before my visit.

The sun streamed through the window on Pereira as he sat up in his bed, the ruffled white sheets strewn about him. He hadn't noticed my entrance and was looking down at his stump in disbelief. He was still suffering from intense shock – the explosion and then the creeping realisation that he had lost his leg and would never walk properly again.

His hands went down to his leg, caressed it gently then they moved up to his face where they covered his eyes as if he were trying to shut out the sight of his broken body. I watched quietly. It was one of the saddest sights I have ever seen.

One of the medics came in and stood next to me. Then he spoke. "How are you feeling?"

Pereira jerked upward as if bringing his mind from a long distance away back to the harsh present. "Very bad . . ." He broke off and put his hands to his head. He looked down at his mutilation again – the hands wandered uncontrollably back to it then back to his face. The motion was repeated and Pereira, for a few moments, looked like a large clockwork figure.

The medic leaned close to him over the bed. "You must be strong; you can still make a life for yourself."

Pereira let out a muffled moan then looked up at us. His eyes had a yellow tinge; watery, frightened, childlike. "I am trying, but it is very bad . . ." He broke off again.

For Pereira, perhaps, it was worse than for some of the other tribesmen who have fallen victim to mines. He was literate. The effort and the determination which gained him an education must have been great. So much greater must have been the agony of realisation that he could only be half a man. And unlike the soldiers, Pereira didn't even qualify for the transistor radio or the 200 escudos a month disability allowance. I left the ward without saying a word; everything had been said for me in Pereira's tortured face.

More than anything else the Portuguese soldiers fear mines. They realise that to tread on one in the bush means the almost certain loss of a limb and other injuries. Dr Bastos, the evasive director of Nampula's military hospital explained it this way: "We have all the equipment we need, but most mine victims have one or both legs amputated because it takes too long to evacuate them from the jungle to the hospital.

"Infections set in quickly in the field and the wounds are usually full of dust and sand. There is nothing we can do about it."

Frelimo realised fully the psychological impact mine warfare had on the average Portuguese soldier and at some stages of the war as many as 200 mines were laid weekly in the northern province of Cabo Delgado alone. Even when the war in Mozambique is long over and forgotten, people – mostly innocent villagers – will be treading on mines in Mozambique.

And the crowning irony of it is that in the same hospitals that the mine victims lie are also some of the men who laid the mines. Lying in the hospitals side by side with sick injured or legless Portuguese soldiers are captured Frelimo guerrillas injured in combat. Outwardly, none of the Portuguese troops shows animosity – all seem to accept the directive that the guerrillas have as much right to treatment as the soldiers.

Although all inmates are treated equally, the irony of the situation is that an injured Frelimo is given preference to a Portuguese soldier when it comes to evacuation from the field. If there is only room for one injured, the Frelimo rebel will be given preference. I met a number of these men in the hospitals and it was a constant source of amazement to me that the men I was talking to had in some cases only days before been ranging in the bush, laying mines and ambushing convoys.

I remember one in particular in Nampula Hospital who had been shot through the leg when his group was caught in an ambush by a group of commandos in Cabo Delgado. He was propped up in bed, pillows behind his back and a delightful young nurse was attending to him. The attendant medic asked him how he was doing.

"Very well, thank you."

"Is there anything you need?"

"Yes. I would like a pen and some writing paper." I wondered to whom his letter would be addressed and what its contents would be, whether the receiver would ever believe that he was in a Portuguese hospital on the road to repair. I noticed, too, he was reading the New Testament in Portuguese; it lay open at Mathew's gospel ". . . Take heed that no man seduce you. For many seduce many. And you shall hear of wars and rumours of wars. See that ye be not troubled. For these things must come to pass . . ."

Portuguese paternalism also extends to her enemies. "They are only misguided," is how one of the doctors explained it. "They are not really to blame. Many of them are press-ganged from the bush to join Frelimo, others are intimidated with threats to themselves or their families. It doesn't take them long to be mentalised to the Frelimo way of thinking because they have no standard of comparison."

This may have been true to an extent, but there seemed to be a certain amount of naiveté among some of the Portuguese about the whole concept of guerrilla warfare.

Perhaps the most lucid explanation of the nature of guerrilla warfare comes from Robert Taber in his definitive work, "The War of the Flea".

"Guerrilla war," writes Taber, "in the larger sense . . . is revolutionary war, engaging a civilian population, against the military forces of established or usurpative governmental authority . . . Ostensible causes can be misleading. Patriotism, race, religion, the cry for social justice: beneath all of these symbolic and abstract 'causes' that have inspired the revolutions of this century, one discovers a unifying principle, a common mainspring.

"It is a revolutionary impulse, an upsurge of popular will, that really has very little to do with questions of national or ethnic identity, or self-determination, or forms of government, or social justice, the familiar shibboleths of political insurgency. It is not even certain that economic deprivation in itself is the decisive factor that it is widely assumed to be. Poverty and oppression are, after all, conditions of life on the planet that have been endured by countless generations with scarcely a murmur.

"The will to revolt, so widespread as to be almost universal today, seems to be something more than a reaction to political circumstances or material conditions. What it seems to express is a newly awakened consciousness, not of 'causes', but of potentiality. It is the spreading awareness of the possibilities of human existence, coupled with a growing sense of the casual nature of the universe, that together inspire, first in individuals, then in communities and entire nations, an entirely new attitude towards life . . .

"The guerrilla is subversive of the existing order in that he is the disseminator of revolutionary ideas; his actions lend force to his doctrine and show the way to radical change. Yet it would be an error to consider him as being apart from the seedbed of revolution. He himself is created by the political climate in which revolution becomes possible, and is himself as much an expression as he is a catalyst of the popular will towards change".

Taber writes – and on the evidence available correctly – that to understand this much about the guerrilla is to avoid two major pitfalls of confusion about the nature of guerrilla warfare.

It is a mistake to believe it is "the offspring of a process of artificial insemination, and that the guerrilla nucleus is made up of outsiders, conspirators, political zombies . . . who somehow stand separate from their social environment while manipulating it to obscure and sinister ends."

The other pitfall was to believe that guerrilla warfare was largely a matter of tactics and techniques, to be adopted by almost anyone who might have need of them, in almost any irregular warfare situation.

Taber's assessment is accurate and very much so in the case of Frelimo, in Mozambique. It would be naive to think that the majority of Frelimo recruits were press-ganged into the movement or terrorised to give their support. The leadership of the organisation is all drawn from the territory and a large number of the members joined the organisation freely of their own choice.

111

The great question, however, is whether the movement has re-tained its initial impetus as a Black Nationalist spearhead to a revo-lutionary awareness in the territory, or whether the Communists have manipulated these initial motives toward new ends.

There is increasing evidence to support the latter theory regarding Frelimo which is heavily reliant on China for moral, ideological and material support. Is the face of Mao Tse-tung hiding cynically behind a Black mask? There is strong evidence to assume it is.

The Portuguese policy of rehabilitating Frelimo guerrillas captured or injured in the bush has not been popular with many of the fight-ing troops, and many of them, who have served in the combat zones, are better versed in the motives of guerrilla warfare than their superiors would believe. As one said to me in Mueda: "Ultimately this is not a terrorist war. That is clearly nonsense. It is at core a revolutionary war and once a man has developed a revolutionary consciousness, no amount of mental rehabilitation will convince him that he hasn't got a right to his place in the sun". That, I thought was a logical and clear appraisal of the situation in Mozambique.

Another disturbing feature of the hospitals in Mozambique's war zones was the lack of equipment. Although many of the doctors I spoke to were adamant that they had all the equipment they needed, this was not so. The problem stemmed largely from the fact that most of the doctors are conscript soldiers. Where one may be trained in the use of one set of equipment, another may not. And the Portuguese cannot continually change existing equipment to meet the whims of each new batch of conscript doctors. The ultimate losers were always the injured.

Despite the claims of the director of the Nampula military hospital that they had all the equipment they needed, a young conscript sur-geon, Dr "Paw Paw" Alemao disproved the claim. We were walking through the hospital's two intensive care units.

Lying in one was a Portuguese soldier who had been shot in the side in a Frelimo ambush. The bullet had passed right though his lungs, kidney and was still lodged in his liver. The doctor had already operated to patch him up, but couldn't remove the bullet until the patient recovered some of his strength. We were allowed to walk into the intensive care unit without donning sterilised clothing or face masks. I noticed one of the medical orderlies who accompanied us was smoking. This would be unheard of in any correctly run hospital,

Chanting crowds at a GUMO rally in Lourenco Marques show their support for Frelimo.—Picture: Mike McCann

Left: Anti-South African and Rhodesian banners displayed during a political rally in Lourenco Marques, capital of Mozambique. —Picture: Courtesy Dennis Gordon *Rand Daily Mail* Africa Bureau.

Right: A political prisoner embraces his wife after being released from the notorious Machava jail in Lourenco Marques after an amnesty was granted by the military junta in Portugal. Picture: Courtesy Mike McCann.

where it is almost impossible even to gain access to an intensive care unit, let alone to smoke in it.

Dr Alemao passed me a note as we went through. All it said was: "Ventilator, Respirator or Bennet or Engstrom". He knew we were from South Africa and probably hoped we would pass his message onto the voluntary organisations in South Africa that provide aid to the Portuguese hospitals in Mozambique. I learnt later that the doctor had his leave curtailed for passing me the message – the Portuguese don't want to give the impression that they are not self-sufficient. The sad fact is they are not.

But not all the injured are combat wounded. I met one fellow in one of the wards who had been savaged by a lion. He was enormously proud of the fact and posed for us, showing us the great welts on his back and arms where the animal had clawed into his flesh.

He had been with a group of Portuguese troops on a march. By nightfall they halted and bedded down for the night. He chose a spot beneath a mopani tree, lay down and let the day's weariness take over. He woke up with a fully grown lion breathing over him. The lion pawed him almost playfully, taking a healthy portion of his left arm with him. In desperation, the terrified man stuck his hand down the lion's throat and grabbed its tongue. It took him a few moments to find his voice and by the time his friends heard his screams, the animal had torn his clothing to pieces and left its claw marks on his back and arms for life. The others arrived and killed it.

There have been a number of incidents like this in the bush of Mozambique, but few of the men attacked by wild animals are as fortunate as that one.

There is one other observation worth noting that indirectly relates to the military hospitals in Mozambique.

Every Saturday afternoon in Nampula, the tribesmen come from miles around with their wooden carvings to sell in the market near the cathedral. The carvings range from the beautifully stylised Maconde Christs to walking sticks and ivory boats. But I noticed a number of little figures carved in wood among the wares displayed by the carvers. Some of them had been carved with only one leg. Perhaps it was my imagination, but I thought at the time, one-legged people had become such a feature of the 10-year war in Mozambique that they had even worked their way into the culture of the place. Why else would a man carve figures with only one leg?

CHAPTER NINE

CAVALRY IN THE BUSH: VILA PERY

Guerrilla war demands many things of the combatants. For the insurgents it requires great determination and privation, for the established forces it requires innovation. The questions always asked by the regular army faced with guerrilla insurgency are: what can we do to stop them? How can we turn their activities to our advantage?

The two questions are important. The truth of it is that in the modern examples of guerrilla war – the French in Algeria and Vietnam, the British in Cyprus and the Americans in Vietnam – conventional military methods have been proved useless. The Portuguese in Mozambique learnt this hard lesson in 10 years of war in the territory.

But the Portuguese tried to answer their military questions. Firstly, they began to establish fortified villages to prevent the local population from being subverted by Frelimo political commissars and to prevent them from giving assistance to the guerrilla forces who needed the locals' support, food and shelter.

Secondly, they integrated their army to instill in their Black population the belief that the war was as much Mozambique's as it was Portugal's; that the responsibility of maintaining the status quo in Mozambique was as much that of the Black inhabitants as it was of the Whites.

They also tried to rehabilitate captured enemies, which must rate as one of the strangest public relations campaigns in history.

This rehabilitation campaign is in itself extraordinary because it led to the establishment of one of Africa's most competent counter – insurgent fighting groups, the Flechas, or Arrows. The Flechas are comprised largely of former guerrillas who have either defected or been captured by the Portuguese. The men are hardened to bush warfare and are intimately aware of the guerrillas' tactics, their quality and their military capabilities.

In Mozambique the first group of Flechas began operating late in 1973. They fell under the DGS, the now disbanded Portuguese secret police, and Flecha recruits were carefully screened by DGS agents before beginning their rigorous training. In Mozambique they operated in the Vila Pery and Beira districts – the strategically important central region of Mozambique that is bordered to the west by Rhodesia and which was the key to the south.

The Flechas had a large degree of success. Led by DGS agents, they built up a reputation for aggressiveness and ruthlessness in pursuit of their enemy. They continued to operate after the coup d'état in Portugal despite the removal of DGS from the picture in Portugal and Mozambique.

These were some of the ways the Portuguese tried to contain the guerrilla threat. Portuguese tactics have been innovative, but even with that flexible attitude to the war, they were under tremendous pressure and Frelimo made considerable headway in its guerrilla campaign.

With the shift in tactics on the Cabora Bassa hydro-electric scheme and the apparent decision not to try to destroy the project, Frelimo groups by-passed Cabora Bassa and the defences surrounding it and carried the war to the central provinces.

As the war crept slowly, but surely southwards, the Portuguese established what they call a cavalry unit as an experimental counter-insurgency arm in the central provinces where the bush is more open and suitable for horse soldiers. The word "cavalry" is used but, strictly speaking, they are virtually mounted infantrymen, but retaining some of the dash and swagger of the cavalry.

The cavalry are stationed at Vila Pery, a medium-sized town on the strategically important railway line from the port of Beira to the Rhodesian border. This railway line was experiencing increased guerrilla attacks, and when I arrived in Vila Pery two passenger trains on the line had been attacked. Most of the Frelimo attacks on the line, however, were against goods trains, and although I could get no official confirmation, I learnt from people in Vila Pery, some of them army officers, that on average one goods train a week was being mined on that railway line.

The cavalry were billeted in the most comfortable army camp I had seen in Mozambique. It was on the fringes of the town beside the railway line and had a touch of class that set it aside from the average army camp. The officers' mess had a bar, television set, picking up Rhodesian programmes, a small but neat library and a lounge filled with contemporary design furniture. Meals included steak and vegetables, which was unusual in the war zones. The cavalry definitely had something extra – and this was reflected in the men's attitude: slightly haughty, elevated and condescending. There was a reason for it. Many of the men in the unit were experienced horsemen, some with reputations for equestrian achievements in Portugal. They were no ordinary soldiers.

When I visited the camp, they were flexing their muscles in the surrounding bush getting ready for the time when they would be fully operational and playing their part in the war. The date for their inclusion in the war effort had not been set and although the men knew they would be fully operational by the year's end they were itching to get into the battle as soon as possible.

The squadron comprised three platoons of 132 horses and was commanded by Captain Rogerio William, a professional soldier and a considerable horseman. Captain William looked deceptively young. About 5 ft 6 in, he looked like one of those army riders at European horse-jumping competitions, well-seated, polished and well-accoutred.

He believed emphatically in the cavalry as an anti-guerrilla weapon. "All we are really doing," he said, "is adapting an old idea to a new set of circumstances. Cavalry groups were used in the closing stages of the war in Vietnam, but the Americans pulled out before they were given a chance to prove themselves. We are not yet operational, but when we are, I am convinced the use of horses will be successful."

The squadron trained daily on a nearby farm, practising their movement formations and tactics against an imaginary enemy. I joined them at the farm, a few kilometres outside Vila Pery, to watch them in action. It was an impressive sight – although seemingly an anachronism in the year 1974. It was like a flashback in history; tanks and armoured cars were a long way away, but here were men and horses together again, and they seemed to like one another's company. In World War II South Africa raised a division of mounted infantry which was stationed at Ladysmith, but with the end of the Somaliland campaign and the shift of the war to the Western Desert it was decided that horses would be no good against tanks.

The war in Poland proved that. My father, who was in the South African division as a member of the 4th mounted Commando Regiment, said it was a sad day when they all said good-bye to their horses. At Vila Pery one section moved in the open bush, the riders protruding from the shoulder-high elephant grass like tree stumps. A second section moved through the thick bush beside a river, concealed from sight. In reserve was the third section, with the commanding officer and the heavier hardwear – a machine gun and 60 mm mortar strapped to the back of one of the reserve horses. Each section was in radio contact with the commanding officer so that he could co-ordinate their movement through the bush and direct the attack on the enemy. The reserve section usually kept to the higher ground to give it a clearer sight of the field of operations.

The sight of a cavalry unit charging down on you, guns blazing has an unsettling effect as if there is nowhere to hide, not even in the high grass or the clumps of thick bush that it breaks into at irregular intervals. Besides the considerable strike power they muster, the horsemen have a tremendous psychological effect on a concealed enemy, from the sound of the galloping horses to the battle cry of the men in the saddles. Firearms had replaced lances and sabres.

A single platoon, usually 38 to 40 horses, can sweep a 400-metre front – four times the area that can be controlled by the same number of infantrymen. They have many other advantages over foot soldiers. They are highly mobile and can be used efficiently to pursue the enemy even through heavy bush.

Horses can operate in the bush for 10 to 15 days living off the veld or being supplied with foodstuffs by helicopter. Troops, therefore, can be carried over long distances where they can also dismount and operate as infantry. The thinking is that they would be fresh whereas the enemy, having been pursued for a number of miles, would be tired and less likely to put up strong resistance.

The Portuguese got the idea of using mounted soldiers in their African wars in 1966 when the first mounted platoon went into operation in Angola. The success of these men and horses was such that three full squadrons, nearly 400 horses, were operating there at the time of writing. The horses used were bought from South Africa and Argentina.

In 1971, the Portuguese Army began studying the application of horse soldiers in Mozambique, but it took over two years to get horses with the right characteristics. They were eventually all bought from a farmer in Rhodesia.

Selection of the horses is of crucial importance. "They really take a beating in the rough bush conditions," said Captain William. "So,

117

firstly, we have to select only those horses we consider to be hardy enough for the conditions. And then we can only choose horses that will respond to a rugged training course which usually takes a full year to complete. They have to get accustomed to explosions and firing from the saddle. We train them to charge at the source of fire. This includes small arms fire and explosives and you will find that after training they will charge into enemy fire without flinching when the rider opens fire from the saddle."

And for the men in the unit, despite the comfort of their quarters, life has a spartan quality. Each man is responsible for his horse and they often work late into the night caring for the horses in addition to the usual duties of cleaning weapons and spit and polish.

They are extremely proud of their military calling and refuse to be photographed out of the saddle unless they are in dress uniform. As one said to me: "If you want photographs, we will change for you. We are not ordinary soldiers, we are specialists."

But there is no parade ground snobbishness about these men in the bush. They often swim rivers with their horses, sleep with them and, it is likely, some of them will die with them for unless Portugal can negotiate a peace with Frelimo and the other guerrilla organisations in Mozambique, these men will have to play their part, just as all the others have for 10 long years.

Also at the Vila Pery military camp is a unit of dog handlers. This, too, was a fairly recent addition to the army. Most of the dogs came from South Africa and their handlers are teaching them how to locate mines by smelling out the explosives. This has been used successfully in South Africa and Rhodesia.

Vila Pery is an interesting town. It was more accommodating to visitors than some of the outlying towns because every year it had experienced the influx of tourists to Mozambique from Rhodesia. Being on the main road and railway between Umtali, in Rhodesia, and the tourist port of Beira, Vila Pery has experienced Rhodesian dollars and got to like them. Visitors are always welcome and even more so now since the tourist traffic has been cut off by guerrilla attacks to the railway and on the road to Rhodesia. Few cars venture along that road these days and even many of the farmers in the district around Vila Pery have left the land to seek the safety of the town. This is one of the reasons for the shortage of fresh vegetables in the area.

A number of the farms near Vila Pery have been attacked by Frelimo groups and hostages are known to have been taken on occasions. I even heard of a White farmer whose two sons were taken by a Frelimo band and have not been heard of since. There was also the case of a five-year-old girl, Maria Ligia Pereira, who was kidnapped in January, 1974, during a Frelimo attack on her parents' home in Cobo Delgado.

News of her came from the International Red Cross which said she was being held in Tanzania and was being well treated. The parents had kept Maria's kidnapping a secret and only told officials when the father, Tome Fernandes Barrao, was brought to Beira Hospital four months later, to have his leg amputated. He had been injured by a Frelimo rocket.

I wanted to write a feature article on the railway from the Rhodesian border to Beira, because, besides being important to tourists, the railway was one of Rhodesia's main outlets to the sea.

After Rhodesia declared UDI on November 11, 1965, the British Government blockaded the port of Beira – with a single warship – in an attempt to prevent imports getting to Rhodesia. It seemed to be more of a token resistance to the illegal regime of Mr Ian Smith, because the presence of that British warship had little or no effect on materials being landed at the port of Beira destined for Rhodesia. In fact, Britain's lonely warship off the coast of Beira had become something of a Rhodesian party joke, but perhaps it gave the British Government something to hold out to the international community as an example of Britain's determination to bring Smith's White minority government to its knees.

Rhodesia became something of a "Waterloo" for Britain's Labour Prime Minister, Harold Wilson, and it emphasised once again the futility of sanctions and the ineptness of politicians who still believe in this weapon. Mr Wilson said after the Rhodesian UDI that the rebel White Government of Rhodesia would be brought to its knees in weeks – that was nine years ago. Since then, Wilson lost a general election, lost face over the EEC and returned once again to 10 Downing Street, largely discredited, and Ian Smith is still thumbing his nose at Britain.

The most dangerous stretch of the railway is from Machipanda, where it crosses into Rhodesia, to Inchope about 100 kilometres down the line to Beira. We decided to ride the train from Vila De

Manica to Gondola, a 70-kilometre stretch along that dangerous section.

The train steamed into the station, where a group of off-duty troops climbed on. A number of Black families climbed aboard with cardboard boxes, blankets, one even had two hens in a small wooden cage.

In the corridors of the carriages, Portuguese militiamen rested their semi-automatics FN rifles out of the windows in case the train was ambushed. The greatest hazard, however, was not ambushes but mines. From the evidence available, most of the mines have been detonated from the nearby bush. The guerrilla groups detonate the mines directly beneath the locomotives.

We walked the length of the train, taking stock of the Portuguese security measures. In the guardsvan there were two machineguns, one trained on the bush on either side of the train. There were also two mortars, both 60 mm. It was only later, as the train laboured through a high cutting along its course, that I noticed a group of commandos in one of the carriages. They were heavily armed.

I spoke briefly to the commander of this little group, nine in all. He was a young White sergeant. After we promised not to take any photographs of the commandos on the train, he relaxed and spoke about his assignment to guard the trains on that run.

"We are only really a reserve. The militiamen guard the trains, but we keep a group of commandos in reserve in case of ambush, because the militia aren't very well trained. Ultimately, we are responsible for the train and the welfare of the passengers," he said.

There were only four Whites on the train besides two of the commandos and the sergeant. One of them was a baby boy aged 18 months. He was lying fast asleep on the lower bunk of one of the first-class compartments. It was quite a strange sight to see a White child fast asleep, the picture of innocence, while just outside in the corridor, a Black militiaman stood with his rifle at the ready to protect the passengers in case of attack.

It made me think about traditional attitudes in South Africa where even during World War II Black troops in the South African Army were only allowed to carry assegais and act as stretcherbearers and batmen. This attitude is now changing.

The trains on that line were being attacked regularly – I learnt, on average, once a week. The Portuguese had found no deterrent to the attacks and already had stopped overnight traffic on the railway, allowing only one train through a day for security reasons.

The crippled locomotives, I was told, were towed back down the line to Beira for repair. I tried to get access to the railway repair workshops in Beira to see the extent of damage to locomotives on the line and try to work out how many were being mined, but was refused permission.

We travelled the stretch of railway without incident and returned to Vila Pery where we were due to catch a flight to Beira the same day. We checked out of our little pension and drove through the palm-flanked streets of Vila Pery to the airport. The scheduled commercial flight we were due to take to Beira had been rescheduled for Monday and as it was only Friday, we decided to hang around the airport building in case we could hitch a lift with a light plane back to Beira.

The rain began to pour down, driving across the grass airstrip in great torrents. The outlook was depressing. My visa for Mozambique was already out of date and Jimmy Soullier's had only two days to run. As we waited, propping up the little airport bar, a young man wearing sunglasses approached us.

"Are you South Africans?" he asked.

"Yes, you could say that."

"Trying to get to Beira?"

"We'd like to if it's possible." I looked at him. He was medium height, wiry build, dressed in an open neck shirt and corduroys. He also spoke Portuguese and his English had the flat intonation of a Rhodesian.

"I'm Peter Caselton," he said extending his hand. We introduced ourselves and waited as he thought for a moment. "I don't think you'll have much luck here, but there's a bus leaving for Beira this evening, perhaps you could chance that." I was a bit unsure what he meant by "chance", but it seemed a better alternative than waiting around the airport building for days.

"Why don't you come back to my place, have something to eat and then I'll take you to the station later on to catch the bus," he said.

We drove back through the streets of Vila Pery. Water gushed from the storm drains and formed rivers down the side of the road, churning the mud up and flowing over the dirt road.

The little suburban houses glinted in the rain: pink, ochre, blue; everything had a sharp, fresh texture. The green lawns shone greener still and the whole place had been transformed from a dull farming town to a neat, tidy little canvas of rich colour.

Peter's Rhodesian wife, Ros, welcomed us and set the tea on the boil as we sat talking about Vila Pery. Peter was a crop-sprayer and had lived there for four years. A number of other crop-sprayers worked out of Vila Pery, but Peter was the only one resident there, hence his working knowledge of Portuguese, which is not an easy language to pick up at the best of times.

"We'll have to leave one of these days," said Peter. "Ros has been wonderful, but it's all a bit unsettling at present. Nobody really knows what is going on and those who do are not likely to tell you."

I told him that one of the army officers at Vila Pery's military camp had mentioned that three GE volunteer troops had been gunned down two days previously on the road from Vila Pery to the Rhodesian border.

Peter looked a bit concerned. "Well that's the first I've heard about it. We have been driving to Umtali once a week to buy vegetables; you can't get them here because most of the farmers have left the land to come into the town. I suppose we'll just have to fly there in future.

"That's the greatest problem at present. You can't get information. They could lose a dozen men on the road and unless an outsider was involved nothing would be said about it. We have to rely on the Rhodesian newspapers to get any information."

Ros, a tall, attractive blonde wearing jeans and a T-shirt, came in with the tea. Perched on her shoulder was a talking cockatiel. Ros and Peter struck me as an adventurous couple. His job was dangerous. Only two months before he had flown in to some high-voltage electricity cables in his aircraft while spraying crops near the town. The tailwheel had caught one of the cables as he pulled up, but too late.

The plane went straight in, nose first. As luck would have it, Peter survived – bruised, scratched and shaken. The pylons carrying the electricity cables had not been cemented into the ground properly and six had been ripped out by the aircraft.

"If those pylons had been installed correctly, I would be dead. So I owe my life to the inefficiency of some Portuguese construction team. It could only have happened in Mozambique," said Peter. He was smiling.

122

The cockatiel jumped on to my shoulder and nibbled away at my ear as we drank our tea.

"It's been interesting living here, but we will probably have to leave soon. It's just too unstable at present. The problem is that I've been paid out in Mozambique escudos, which are valueless outside the territory," said Peter.

Ros interrupted: "Would you like to change your shirt?" she asked. I looked at her smiling face. She was talking to me.

"Not really, Why?" I hadn't thought the weeks in the bush had left that much mark.

"The cockatiel has crapped all over your back. Sorry." The casual nature of the remark by this smiling woman caught me unawares. The others were laughing.

I changed my shirt and then it was time to leave for the bus station. The short time we had spent with Peter and Ros impressed us both. It was also a diversion for them to entertain strangers, but they showed us warm hospitality which is a common feature among Rhodesians and South Africans who live outside the big cities.

There are a number of crop-sprayers throughout Mozambique. I found them to be a useful source of information as they have no axe to grind and travel extensively around the territory. They are also in constant contact with other commercial pilots, and between them they have built up their own information network because of the lack of news in Mozambique.

It was a crop-sprayer who told me about the first attack on civilian trucks travelling on the road between Lourenco Marques and the port of Beira. There had been no guerrilla activity along that road until then and the attack had an unsettling effect on the White civilian population in the area, especially those living in Beira.

The people of Beira had already demonstrated outside the provincial governor's house because of the Frelimo attacks on the railway lines leading out of the port to Rhodesia and Malawi. After one of these attacks, the shopowners in Beira and Vila Pery had closed their shops in protest. Because of the censorship of news, they had no idea how far Frelimo bands had penetrated into the central provinces, and the attacks on the railway lines, so close to the two towns, had come as a shock. When the Beira-Malawi train was machine-gunned, killing a ticket inspector and two soldiers, the residents of the town of Inhaminga, 188 kilometres north of Beira, were so enraged that a number of them, mostly women and children, lay across the tracks as a protest, preventing trains from continuing to Malawi.

But the first attack on the road leading south from Beira to the capital of Lourenco Marques must have had a far greater shock quality. My pilot informant told me sometime after the attack that the bodies of three White Portuguese truck drivers had been taken to Vila Pery rather than Beira, probably in case there was a reaction from the residents of Beira, already known for their dissatisfaction at the protection given them by the army.

"There were three of them. I saw the bodies brought in. All three had had their hearts cut out and one had had the back of his skull cracked open like a nut. The brains had been removed.

"Apparently three trucks had been ambushed and raked with machinegun fire. One was a milk truck, another a beer truck. I don't know what the third one was. But it seems the guerrillas had ambushed them and then got drunk on beer before hacking the bodies in the way they did."

There is a reason for not mentioning the source of some of the stories. When I left Mozambique, I wrote a story mentioning some of the things Peter Caselton told me. On a later visit to Mozambique I met Peter again in Nampula. He told me he had been visited by DGS, the secret police, shortly after publication of the story in South Africa.

"I told them to get lost," said Peter. "It could, however, have been nasty if what I told you wasn't true, but it was, so they didn't really have a leg to stand on."

Although the DGS has been disbanded since the coup in Portugal, I would not like there to be any recriminations against any of the pilots I spoke to. For that reason names have been withheld.

One told me how on one occasion his light aircraft was commandeered by the Portuguese army to fly troops to the famous Gorongosa Game Reserve, which is situated midway between Vila Pery and Beira.

"I flew them to the park not knowing what it was all about. It was only when we got there that I learnt there had been a Frelimo attack in the park the previous night. I was quite staggered to see that the authorities hadn't closed the park. The tourists were still driving about snapping shots of game. They obviously knew nothing about the attack and, presumably, the authorities didn't want to tell them in case it affected the tourist trade to the reserve," he said. This was another strange example of the Portuguese reluctance to keep people informed about the military situation.

One of the more gruesome incidents related to me was the experience of a young commercial pilot who had to fly into a tiny airport serving the town of Canxixe, north of the Gorongosa Game Reserve.

He had flown in to drop some supplies. At the airport building he noticed the whole place was pervaded with the smell of decay. He asked one of the men at the airport the reason and he was taken to the back of the building where 12 bodies were lying in the shade. Why weren't they buried,? he asked.

"The guy said they had to wait for the papers before the bodies could be buried. Apparently they were all from Portugal and the authorities had to wait for permission before they could be buried in Mozambique soil," said the pilot. "The Portuguese are pretty taken with bureaucracy, but that was a bit much."

Like Peter Caselton, the crop-sprayer in Vila Pery, a number of people in Mozambique are holding Mozambique escudos and cannot leave the territory until they find a way of getting rid or them or exchanging them for a viable currency. According to another pilot, one of the ways of overcoming the problem was by going to Beira to buy outboard engines which were free from excise duties.

"Today you can't buy an outboard engine in Beira because they must have got wise to it. Guys were buying them then taking them to Rhodesia and reselling them for Rhodesian dollars," the pilot said. This strange band of men, the crop-spraying pilots of Portuguese East Africa, have many interesting stories to tell about Mozambique. Some are credible; others could have been embroidered.

Here is one example. A Black passenger on one pilot's flight offered to sell him an assortment of shrunken heads. One was that of a young White woman. The price: 3 000 escudos. "I didn't know who the guy was, nor did I want to. My job was to fly him not to question him," said the pilot.

We said good-bye to Peter Caselton at the bus station and climbed aboard. It was packed: women, children, animals. One character had a basket of fish. With a White woman and her daughter, we were the only Whites on the bus. It was still raining and all the windows were closed. I thought of a recent statement by Mrs Betsy Verwoerd, widow of the late South African Prime Minister, Dr H. F. Verwoerd. Mrs Verwoerd had said that the African had a distinct smell, a statement which offended many White South Africans and Blacks. Poor Betsy Verwoerd! How would she have reacted if she had been with us on our cramped five-hour journey in that particular multiracial bus?

It was the most amazing bus ride of my life. At one stage, after driving past miles of fairly dense bush, a man appeared in the middle of the road as though spirited from the undergrowth. The bus stopped and the burly Black driver hauled himself with difficulty from the driver's seat and doffed his straw hat. The man in the road got in and started inspecting tickets. His action had a fantasy quality. He was rewarded by discovering a "stowaway" whom he promptly kicked off the bus before getting off himself and disappearing back into the bush. The unfortunate "stowaway" was left standing by the side of the road, the rain falling down on him and his miserable little collection of possessions as we continued into the sunset.

Every now and then the bus would draw into a siding and a passenger would alight or a new one climb aboard. On one occasion an elderly White got on with his little Coloured daughter. He was wearing a pith helmet and a safari suit, and while he fell asleep on the seat his daughter crawled under the seat and slept on the floor.

Sitting next to me was a raw African woman. She had deep scars on her cheeks and a type of mudpack in her hair, which made it stick up every which way as if a mad hairdresser had translated his nightmare into a hairstyle. In her arms she cradled a child and when it woke up she thrust one of her breasts into its mouth before it could begin to howl. The movement was entirely impersonal as though she were tucking into a waistband a loose corner of a domestic apron. It was sundown when the bus conductor stepped over the blankets, baskets and bodies in the aisle and spoke to the driver. He stopped the bus and again went through the laboured routine of dragging his enormous body out of the seat. Then the men went down the aisle, and for some unknown reason, I thought they were about to throw Jimmy Soullier and me off the bus.

They stopped over a small, shrivelled old African. The conductor made a face and grabbed the old man's basket away from him and opened it to show the driver. As he lifted the lid, the distinct smell of rotten inkfish drifted down the aisle like an evil wind. The old man was thrown off the bus to stand in the road with his stinking hand

126

luggage and watch the bus's rear lights disappear down the road. Not even the rain, however, could have cooled off those inkfish.

We made further progress, and after a time the bus halted once more. Outside, through the sheets of rain, I could see the flooded road water. In front of us a civilian truck was labouring through the torrent in the road. The water was up to the mudguards. We inched along for over an hour. The road was indistinguishable, a lake of water stretching as far as I could see on both sides of the bus.

I was attracted by a movement near the man in the sun helmet. It was his daughter, the little Coloured girl, who had woken and left the security of her hiding place under the seat. She was opening Jimmy's camera bag. His reaction amazed me. He reached down and retrieved his bag kindly, dug about inside and brought out a spool of film, which he gave to the little girl. Here was Christian charity, a generous gesture considering the value of the cameras and that she might have damaged them.

"Hope she chokes on it," mumbled Jimmy. Then, putting his bag on his lap he went back to sleep. Christian Charity!

We were both asleep when the bus eventually chugged into Beira. The rain was still pouring down and the streets were aflood.

We booked into a hotel, showered and soon went back to sleep. The next morning, we learnt, sections of the road had been washed away. We had just made it.

CHAPTER TEN

THE AIR FORCE GENERAL: BEIRA

The atmosphere of uncertainty and insecurity in Beira was almost tangible. The White residents were anxious about the inroads made by Frelimo into the central provinces and were not slow to show their disapproval of the army's efforts to protect them. It was the first time a major city had been threatened with direct attack in the history of the war.

For the first time, too, responsible commentators on African affairs began to sound warnings in the South African Press. Foremost among them were Wilf Nussey, Editor of the *Star's* Africa News Service and Dennis Gordon of the *Rand Daily Mail* Africa Bureau. Wilf Nussey knows the territory intimately and was immediately aware of the implications of the Frelimo thrust southwards.

In an authoritative article in the Johannesburg *Star* he wrote in February: "Since New Year the big Rhodesian tourist traffic to Beira and the famed Gorongosa Game Reserve has been chopped to almost nothing by the triple axes of cholera, petrol rationing and terrorism.

"But even if they did not need cholera shots or petrol coupons, few Rhodesians would, as one put it, 'risk my wife's and kid's necks by driving there through a lot of terrorists'.

"Tourism accounts for 20 per cent of Beira's revenue. Most comes from the port and railways, now seriously menaced by bombings of the lines to Rhodesia and Malawi.

"Beirans reacted with horror and anger to the attacks on the railways and on the Inhaminga barracks only 180 kilometres to the north. Nobody warned them what to expect – which is astonishing because the signs were clear in the first half of last year (1973).

"Now the authorities caught unawares, are scrambling to patch together a defence line all the way from Beira to the Rhodesian frontier. They may be too late because the Frelimo southward thrust is accompanied by effective new tactics.

"When, from 1970, they began infesting the great, raw Tete salient from Zambia while the Portuguese were preoccupied in the Cabo

The terrible aftermath of the alleged Frelimo attack on Inhacamba, a village 80 km south of the town of Tete.

Two more pictures of the massacre.

Delgado and Niassa war zones, the Frelimo depended considerably on willing or co-erced support from African villagers.

"They still infest Tete but local support has been largely denied to them by the massive resettlement of the locals in big protected towns. Thus the Frelimo began their present campaign of terrorising these towns while they infiltrated south. They first sent down subversive agents to win over Africans in the untouched areas, plus a steady stream of arms and supplies – all packed down on porters' backs.

"When a Spanish surgeon was shot dead north of the Gorongosa Game Reserve early last year, and the Gorongosa camp was shot up, Portuguese paratroops were rushed in.

"They found that the Frelimo had been there for a year or more before the first trigger was pulled, that most of the locals were pro-Frelimo and that the few small Frelimo gangs operating in the area simply melted away into the population. Once the shooting had started, Frelimo incidents began occurring at the frightening rate of 15 to 20 a month, building up to the present onslaught.

"If this Frelimo pattern is continuing (and there is no reason to believe it is not) then by now their advance agents are already blazing the trail for killing far south of the Beira-Rhodesia railway – possibly south of the Save River and approaching the Transvaal."

A grave warning indeed.

The signs were clear. Frelimo had caught the Portuguese completely on the wrong foot in the central provinces and the psychological effect these attacks were having so far south was enormous. South Africa and Rhodesia were suddenly on the brink of involvement. For Rhodesia the position was clearly far more serious than South Africa. Already 70 per cent of the Rhodesian frontier with Mozambique was infiltrated by Frelimo, and ZANU (Zimbabwe African National Union) guerrilla groups were launching attacks from Mozambique into northeast Rhodesia, notably the Centenary and Mount Darwin areas.

The ZANU groups were using established Frelimo infiltration routes from Zambia through the Tete district where Frelimo had by-passed the Cabora Bassa Dam into the central provinces. This made it easy for ZANU groups to act as fellow travellers with Frelimo before infiltrating into the north-eastern regions of Rhodesia. The Rhodesian Government had already admitted that Rhodesian troops had crossed into Mozambique in hot pursuit of ZANU guerrilla bands which had launched attacks in Rhodesia.

It had become possible for ZANU to attack areas in Rhodesia far south of Centenary and Mount Darwin. Using Frelimo infiltration routes through Mozambique, ZANU groups could launch attacks anywhere along the 70 per cent of the Rhodesian border that Frelimo had infiltrated in Mozambique. It was simply a matter of crossing the Rhodesian border, attacking a target, and returning to Mozambique where they could disappear among the local people who were friendly to Frelimo. Rhodesia was also in a diplomatic and political strait-jacket. In the eyes of the international community, she was ruled by an illegal regime and she was walking a political tightrope. If Rhodesian troops operating in Mozambique in hot pursuit of ZANU groups should have made any mistakes and attacked Frelimo groups, or even local villagers – which often happens in this kind of warfare – the international community would have put considerable pressure on Rhodesia.

Portugal, too, could ill afford an overt military relationship with Rhodesia. Not only was Portugal dedicated to the principle of multiracialism, which was anathema to the White supremist Government of Mr Ian Smith in Rhodesia, but Portugal could not afford a direct relationship with an illegal regime in Rhodesia. Portugal was already under considerable fire from the international community and her delicate membership of the North Atlantic Treaty Organisation (NATO) could not be strained further by linking arms with Rhodesia.

For South Africa, the deteriorating military situation in the central provinces of Mozambique was less drastic. But already Frelimo military groups were operating as far south as the Save River, only 190 kilometres from the South African border. The north eastern border between South Africa and Mozambique is a weak point in South African strategic arrangements. A vast and almost totally unpoliced area runs parallel to the Mozambique border in the north-eastern Transvaal. It comprises the Kruger National Park, the world-renowned game park, and the Black Homeland of Gazankulu, the home of the Shangaan people.

The best way to gauge South African concern with the southward thrust of Frelimo in Mozambique is to consider that in the previous year one of the largest exercises of South African troops since World War II was held in Gazankulu. It involved a full brigade of non-conventional warfare regiments.

I was fortunate enough to accompany the troops on that exercise and I was also in touch with a number of game rangers in the Kruger National Park who were showing concern with the situation in Mozambique. Some of them had already established a commando for protection in case of infiltration into the park from Mozambique. They were fully aware of the possible implications of Frelimo's southward thrust in Mozambique. It was quite feasible that the African National Congress (ANC), the outlawed South African Black Nationalist organisation, could follow the example of ZANU and use established Frelimo infiltration routes through Mozambique to launch attacks into South Africa.

Judged on the reaction of a large section of the South African public to Sharpeville, when a number of Blacks were shot by the South African Police in 1960, it would only need one guerrilla attack on one of the rest camps in the Kruger National Park virtually to kill the tourist trade to the reserve.

So the direct threat to South Africa was not so far removed as at first it seemed.

Beira, certainly, had a depressed look, and it wasn't only the rain. There is something in the air that cannot be described in Beira. It was a type of festering concern, a looking into an insecure future and pre-occupation with rumour. This was not surprising considering the lack of news that was upsetting the local residents. But we had to get out of Mozambique and there was no time to get to the core of Beiran thinking.

We were sitting at the airport terminal waiting for a flight to Lourenco Maiques. The terminal was packed: troops waiting for connecting flights to the central and northern provinces, their kitbags over their shoulders; and crowds of local residents who had come to meet the TAP jumbo jet from Lisbon. I noticed, too, a large number of senior officers, mostly Air Force men.

Co-inciding with the arrival of the TAP jumbo was the landing of a Portuguese Air Force Boeing 707, also from Lisbon. The passengers came through Customs and Immigration to greet friends and relatives. It was reminiscent of the scenes you see at any international airport around the world – with a difference.

"Who's that?" asked Jimmy, pointing to a middle-aged man in uniform, who had just walked into the terminal.

"Could be the jumbo pilot," I said.

131

"No, there's no other crew members with him."

I looked again. He was an extremely good-looking man; dark, keen eyes, rugged complexion. He stood with his hands behind his back talking to a group of Air Force officers. Hovering in the background were two very attractive Portuguese girls, aged around 18 to 20. On his chest were four full rows of medal ribbons and he had an aura of natural charisma that centered all attention around him.

"I think it's Neto," said Jimmy groping for his cameras. "Did you see he's got three stars on his sleeve? It's General Neto. I'm sure of it."

We got up and approached him through the crowd. As I got near, he was kissing the two girls with a paternal type of affection and the officers had taken a back seat.

I tapped him on the shoulder. "Excuse me, are you General Neto?"

He turned around abruptly and looked at me. I was amazed at the sharpness of his eyes as he searched my face.

"Yes," he said.

We had chased the general half way across Mozambique and given up hope we would ever see him. This chance meeting at Beira Airport was one of those million-to-one chances that seem to happen so regularly with journalists.

We rushed him away upstairs for a cup of coffee and a brief interview. His arrival back from Lisbon held no significance for me at the time, but after the interview I wasn't so sure. A number of rumours had been circulating in Nampula when we were last there that indicated General Neto was on the move. One of them was that he was to take over as commander-in-chief of the armed forces, which at the time seemed ridiculous, but as it turned out was not. It was just an indication of the forces at play in the Mozambique I saw.

I asked the general what he had been doing in Lisbon. His answer set the tone for the future, for on April 25 General Neto was to become No. 3 in the military junta that ruled Portugal after the military takeover. "I was in Lisbon to choose officers," said the general.

General Diogo Neto was already a folk hero in Mozambique, and the reputation he had built up in Nampula where he flew combat missions in his own personal jet, had followed him throughout the territory. I was interested to hear what this dashing airman had to say about the war and the future of Mozambique.

Here is my question-and-answer interview with the general.

"I believe you have strong personal ideas on how the war in Mozambique should be won, would you please comment?"

"It is very difficult to define precisely how the war can be won, but there are a few obvious steps that should be taken. Firstly, we must continue to develop a sophisticated intelligence network both inside Mozambique and outside the territory. Personally, I would like to bomb Frelimo base camps in Tanzania, but the politicians won't allow it.

"Since Frelimo have attacked a number of towns there is a great need for immediate counter-attack measures. If we can develop immediate counter-attacks, Frelimo, will be more reluctant to attack the same targets again.

"It is also difficult to detect the enemy. However, we sometimes know where their bases are because of the missile sites. When we do know this, we must attack them with our full capabilities.

"Parallel to this, the civilian administration should play their part by detecting enemy networks and prevent further internal infiltration. The populations must be concentrated for control, even in places like Beira and Lourenco Marques. If this is done we will have created areas without people, which will make Frelimo's task far more difficult." This answer was interesting in the twin criticisms the general was making. It appeared to me he was criticising the army and the civilian administration.

I then asked him whether the Mozambique Air Force was strong enough to cope with the Frelimo threat.

"It will never be strong enough. We desperately need more and better aircraft for all phases of the air war. Even if we get them, however, we will still need more."

"General, I believe Frelimo is about to use the 'Strella' ground-to-air missile system in the north, when do you expect it to be used?"

"It is natural they will have 'Strella' sooner or later. There is nothing that can prevent it, especially near the borders with Tanzania."

"Yes, but when will 'Strella' be here in Mozambique?"

The general smiled: "It is imminent".

This was the closest I had got to an outright answer regarding the Russian SAM 7 (code name "Strella") missile system's use in Mozambique. I had information that this portable ground-to-air missile was already smuggled into Mozambique from Tanzania and that the first group of 40 Frelimo recruits trained in the missiles' use were due to return from Russia in March.

"Strella" had been used against the Portuguese in Guinea with dramatic results. It was also the "Strella" missile system that had caused such damage to the American Air Force in Vietnam. Highly mobile and easy to handle, this missile homes in on the heat of an aircraft's engines. The Americans had devised a counter-system against the missile in Vietnam. A light on the pilot's instrument panel would show when the missile was in pursuit. The pilot could then scramble the missile's path with a sophisticated electronic device in the aircraft. But the Portuguese had nothing of that nature, and all their aircraft, as well as the DETA jets, were highly vulnerable to the weapon.

It was only in May that the first Portuguese aircraft was shot down with a "Strella". At the time I was in Nampula and couldn't get official confirmation of the attack. It came one week later when the news was broken that a Dakota had been hit flying in Cabo Delgado. The pilot, however, had landed the aircraft at a tiny airstrip without injury to any of the passengers.

Aboard the aircraft was Major Willem Kempen, assistant military attache at the South African Embassy in Lisbon. He was in a party of American, British and Brazilian military attaches on an orientation tour of Mozambique.

Major Kempen described the attack as follows: "There were 13 of us in the aircraft. Being hit by a missile was the last thing on earth – or in the sky – that we expected. There was a sound that can only be described as 'voop'. The next minute there was a roar of the slipstream tearing through a gaping hole in the starboard wing and past a shattered window."

The "Strella" (Russian for Arrow) can easily be carried by two men or even one if the need arises. It is about one metre long and can be extremely dangerous to light aircraft or helicopters up to a height of 3 000 metres. It also poses a threat to larger aircraft on approach to landing or directly after takeoff.

Aircraft travelling at more than 800km/h are safe from the missile as it has to be fired behind the plane so that it can beam in on the heat discharge of the engine exhausts or jets.

It does not have a particularly big charge and is crude, but it is easy to operate and is an ideal weapon for guerrilla warfare.

I continued my interview with General Neto asking him if the military situation in Mozambique had deteriorated.

"The military situation is not really deteriorating. The enemy has no capacity to make large strikes, only small attacks in isolated areas. However, he has the capability of spreading subversion over large areas; this cannot be stopped. It is out of military control and in the lap of the civilian administration," he said. Again he was critical of the civilian administration.

I asked him about the possibility of aid for Portugal's war. His answer was a warning.

"We expect aid from no one. But a very dangerous situation has arisen. Everyone is aware of Communist backing for Frelimo, a situation from which there is no reversal and a situation which naturally is of great concern to us."

"Do you foresee South Africa fighting a guerrilla war in the near future?"

"It depends on the terrain and on what efforts South Africa has taken to try to control the local population. They are an enemy without a face and they are probably in South Africa already waiting for the time to pull the first trigger."

We left General Neto to catch our plane to Lourenco Marques. I was not to see him again until nearly two months later when he returned to Mozambique after another trip to Lisbon as the No. 3 man in the Portuguese military junta headed by Antonio de Spinola.

We had one day in Lourenco Marques before leaving Mozambique and returning to Johannesburg. We lounged about the kerbside cafes taking in the atmosphere and getting our thoughts in order for our return.

That evening Jimmy Soullier phoned his wife for the first time in nearly a month. He had told her before leaving Johannesburg that he was going on a big-game hunting expedition in Mozambique and wouldn't be able to phone her. He had hoped in this way to quell any worries she might have about him. But in the month we had been away, Mozambique had suddenly become a focal point of interest in South Africa. The newspapers were full of reports on Frelimo activity and speculation about the future of the war.

The waiting had been too much for Jimmy's wife and she burst into tears when he finally got through to Johannesburg. She had been sick with worry and when I looked back on our travels, I thought she had a right to be.

We decided to crown our last evening in Mozambique with a good seafood meal. We found a little restaurant near the "Street of Trouble" and set to. With a touch of bravado, I ordered a plate of inkfish. When they served the octopus half an hour later, Jimmy politely excused himself and went to sit at another table. I can't say I blamed him, the plate of food before me gave off a nauseating smell. Rather than lose face I took a bite and excused myself to join Jimmy.

The waiter was undaunted and came over with the menu. "You don't like?" he asked with a slightly pained expression, as if the inkfish were listening in on the conversation.

"Well, I've never tried it before . . ." The waiter smiled widely and disappeared into the back with the inkfish, only to return a few minutes later with a plate of grouper – and delicious it was. When we got the bill later in the evening, the inkfish did not feature, a gesture which earned the waiter an enormous tip. It was no use taking escudos back to South Africa. It certainly made the waiter's night and, as Jimmy said: "There we all were having a real good time."

We sat watching the people go by, our work almost over. I looked at Jimmy. He looked past me saying nothing. When I turned, I saw another perhaps worthier of receiving some escudos. It was a young Black beggar, his two arms sticking way out of a tattered jacket like dorsal fins on a fish. He looked like a thalidomide child, the two little stumps waving about from beneath the jacket. I decided then I had had enough of Mozambique.

I slipped a 50-escudo note into his top pocket. He bowed and walked off into the lighted street. I watched him go, wondering whether he was a war victim or whether he had been born that way. As he reached the corner I saw a group of ragged Black children move out of the shadows and knock him to the ground. He lashed out at them with his feet, those two stumps thrashing helplessly at the air. I was willing him to fight them off, but it was hopeless, even with arms he would have been no match for them. A grubby hand reached into his top pocket and took the crumpled note, and by the time Jimmy and I were on the scene they had disappeared into the shadows.

He lay unmoving on the ground. I noticed other diners had seen the incident. Nobody had stirred.

Other more cabable hands eventually took charge of the assaulted youth.

PART TWO

A view of Cabora Bassa, the giant hydro-electric scheme being built near Songo in Tete Province. When completed this project will be the fourth largest of its kind in the world.—Picture: James Soullier.

Lisbon sends
in th

All roads lea
to Frelimo
in Mozambiqu

Diary of
nounting
violence

to be a
second
Algeria

From
GRAHAM LINSCOTT
(of The Argus Africa
News Service)

**LOURENCO
MARQUES.** —
After nearly half a
century of dormancy
enforced by Portugal's
dictatorship, the 300-
000 - square - mile
territory of Mozam-
bique is abruptly be-
ginning to change —
like the chrysalis of
some obscure African
insect.

THURSDAY: Mass rall/
of/ Frelimo at Machava
Posters of Samor:
Machel. Whites stay away

FRIDAY: Another un
scheduled rally brings LM
to standstill. Even bigge:
crowd at Machava vows to
stay there till in
dependence granted. At
night: Newspapers
Noticias and Tribuna
stoned by White crowd
offices of pro-Frelimo democrats set alight.

SATURDAY: Thirty
thousand Blacks at
Machava acclaim Frelimo
settlement in Lusaka.
Whites demonstrate in car
cavalcades. Newspapers
again stoned. Whites
storm central prison and
release political and
criminal prisoners. Radio
Club stormed and oc-
cupied.

SUNDAY: MFM formed.
Plans to announce in-
dependence.

'Tense' SA eyes
Frelimo

PRETORIA. — The power
handover to Frelimo in
Mozambique — and the
ritory — are bristling with
growing chaos in the ter-
uncertainties for South
Africa.

Africa would
cording to dipl
servers, on the
movement is
by communist
African forces.

Machel: We
will crush
Mozambique's
Whites are
rebels
on the move

Cape Times Correspondents and Sapa

-ES-SALAAM.—The Frelimo leader Mr Samora Mache
night that his troops had linked with Portuguese forc
he major towns of Mozambique to combat the "Whit

Fears of another Congo

"While we are sitting on a volcano, our people
are debating the sex of the angels as the
Christians were doing when Constantinople
was about to fall to the Turks," a leading
government official in Lourenco Marques
old TO THE POINT's Hans Germani last week.

He was mocking the unrealistic stream of
debates, discussions, strikes and demands
with which the whites of the Mozambique

**MOZAMBIQUE –
SPECIAL REPORT**

Gomes adamantly stressed his optimism
about Angola remaining Portuguese while he
was doubtful about Mozambique. Politicians
of the Movement of Democrats of Mozam-

mobilise blacks. The respected newspaper,
Diario, did not appear on the streets one day
when its employees, demanding a 50 per cent
increase, attempted a takeover.

In the flotsam of parties fighting among
themselves, three major groups have emerged:
□ GUMO, led by ex-terrorist woman leader
Joana Simao, commanding the support of the
powerful two million strong Macue tribe, and
by Lourenco Marques businessman Jorge
Abreu. Originally standing for autonomy, this
group now wants to join Frelimo for independence

destroy
(in-
reement
e the
n the
al and

very quickly neu
and annihilated."
The Portu
leadership, in
President Spinola
guaranteed it wou
here to and ful
plement last Sat
Lusaka accords se
ou that   ing a transitional
bandits,   government til
r e-   dependence on Jt
will be   next year.

What are prospects under Frelimo

The headlines tell the story.

Either way, the passing of Mondlane saw the end of an era in the Mozambique war and the beginning of another – backed to the hilt by the Chinese. The Russian star was already waning.

His passing was a severe setback for the Black nationalist forces. His death deprived the nationalists of a pre-eminently able freedom fighter leader. In many ways the tragedy of his death is only really being felt now since the coup in Portugal. Mondlane could have been a great constructive statesman under a self-governing Mozambique.

For a time Frelimo was disrupted in the power struggle for leadership that followed Mondlane's death. Temporary leadership was in the hands of an uneasy triumvirate of Uriah Simango, Lazaro Kavandame and Samora Moises Machel.

Uriah Simango was later expelled along with his supporters as extremists – and Kavandame, surprisingly, defected to the Portuguese.

Samora Machel, a founder member of Frelimo and formerly head of military activities, was appointed president and Marcelino Dos Santos his deputy.

A former male nurse from Lourenco Marques, Machel is a hard-line Communist, trained in Algeria and Russia, though his organisation is dominated by Maoist cadres.

With the coming to power of Machel, the Communist influence in Frelimo was more than a propaganda bogy, and Chinese influence in the movement was dominant.

Observers believe that Marcelino Dos Santos is the last remaining pro-Soviet executive member of Frelimo. But he is politically weak, is distrusted by the Chinese and has the added liability of being married to a White South African girl.

If we are to believe the statements of Frelimo defectors and study the organisation of Frelimo, Machel is virtually a dictator. Frelimo is organised like a military dictatorship. (For Frelimo organisation at a superior level, see appendix three).

This is interesting if you study the general aspects and objectives of Frelimo. These I list below.

General Aspects
Definition: Frelimo is a political organisation constituted among the Mozambique people without distinction of sex, ethnic origin or religious belief or local domicile.

Objectives:
1. Total liquidation in Mozambique of any Portuguese colonial domination and all vestiges of colonialism and imperialism.
2. Winning the immediate independence of Mozambique.
3. Defence and realisation of all aspirations of all the people of Mozambique exploited and oppressed by the Portuguese colonial regime.

Processes of action:
1. Uniting all people in Mozambique.
2. Organisation and mobilisation of all people in Mozambique.

Principles of organisation: Democratic centralisation.
Political orientation: Moderate and non-aligned.

By its structure, Frelimo is certainly not a model of democratic centralism (the basis of which is that the Party and the State are the same; both rest on the people's will, and they must be democratically consulted in the formation of policy), and its political orientation has not been non-aligned.

Frelimo is now faced with its major test. The organisation has been offered sanctuary in Mozambique to establish itself as a political party. It will be interesting to see whether Frelimo will emerge in Mozambique with its stated general aspects intact.

Frelimo is the real power among the guerrilla movements operating in Mozambique, but it is not alone. Another movement worth mentioning is COREMO, referred to in an earlier chapter.

Coremo was formed in 1965 from a number of small groups not in sympathy with Frelimo. Headed by Paul Gumane, Coremo claims that nine of its central committee of 14 are based inside Mozambique and that it has more than 5 000 active members operating mainly in the Tete district.

In fact, there are a number of guerrilla movements on the Mozambique scene. (For a detailed list see appendix four). This factor is significant. Many of these groups are a result of ideological infighting within Frelimo and personality conflicts among the various guerrilla leaders. This may have considerable political implications in the future of Mozambique. It is quite possible that an independent Mozambique will be torn apart by the old feuds among the guerrilla leaders, each of whom has shown in the past that he wanted a slice of the leadership pie. As many of the movements are tribally based, these conflicts could lead to violent tribal conflict in the future.

If the guerrilla movements accept Portugal's proposals and enter Mozambique as political parties, the consequent electoral battle will be a strong indication of how far the guerrilla leaders have gone to patch up their differences.

CHAPTER TWELVE

THE ANATOMY OF A REVOLUTION

It was 15 minutes past midnight, April 25, 1974. Late night radio listeners were astonished to hear a certain record being played that had not been heard for as long as most could remember.

The song was "Grandola, vila morena" (Grandola, the parched town) and its words spoke of "land of fraternity" and "equality on each face" – words that had been banned in Right-wing Portugal for over 40 years.

But what the late night listeners didn't know was that the banned song was a signal, for as the song broke the stuffy air of dictatorship that morning, the first rebel tanks moved toward Lisbon and Portugal's "gentle revolution" was underway. When they woke up on April 25, 1974, the people of metropolitan Portugal sniffed the sweet air of political freedom for the first time in nearly 50 years. People danced in the streets, motorcar horns rocked the ancient capital heralding a new dawn; champagne and wine flowed freely, prim Portuguese girls uncharacteristically blew kisses at the rebel soldiers or stuck flowers in the barrels of their rifles. It was like a political fairytale.

Only four people died for Portugal's new-found freedom that early morning, victims of the hated DGS, the extreme Right-wing Portuguese secret police, who had terrorised or bludgeoned the population for decades and who on that April morning suddenly became the hunted.

It was a great day for liberty and the oldest political adage, that the people will always find freedom from oppression, seemed to be the rule of the day.

For most Portuguese, it was the first time they could speak their minds freely without fear of recriminations, the first time they could read a newspaper and know it was uncensored and the first time they could think about the age-old game of politics and how it affected their lives.

That was a monumental freedom, a heady release from a dictatorship that stretched back to 1932, when Antonio de Oliveira Salazar first put a mailed fist over Portugal and brought that semi-feudal land into the grip of an autocratic, Right-wing dictatorship where democratic freedoms became but a faint, almost inaudible whisper from the past or fleeting, imaginary peep into the future.

Salazar exiled political opponents, maintained a feared political police force and enforced Press censorship. He tolerated no opposition to his determination to retain Portuguese African and other overseas possessions.

The Salazar era stretched to 1968 when he was succeeded by Marcello Jose Alves Caetano. The new Prime Minister was a Salazarist in his political ideas; which were his advocacy of the corporate state as the answer to parliamentary democracy, his strong Catholicism and his fear of Communism at home and abroad as the major threat to the Christian civilisation of the West.

In fact, Caetano was selected by the tri-cornered military, business and Roman Catholic Church establishment as the man least likely to change things.

But Caetano, a former law professor, could read the winds of change and he did institute some changes: easing of Press censorship, regularisation of the legal position of clandestine emigrants, widening of electoral suffrage and the abolition of the previous law demanding Government approval for elected trade-union representatives. But even this was not enough and Portugal still laboured under a dictatorial yoke.

Where Salazar and Caetano were not at odds, however, was over the question of Portugal's African provinces. On the African issue, Caetano was committed to the wars in Africa as the only way of retaining the provinces.

When, suddenly, Caetano's Government was overthrown on April 25, it was no wonder that most people in the free world were amazed at the developments in Portugal and not the least of them the people living in Portugal's far-flung African provinces, where in the case of Mozambique, they had known war for a full 10 years.

To them, Portugal was the only political oracle, steadfast and immovable like the Rock of Gibraltar. Political speculation for the average Mozambican was an alien quality because, for nearly 500 years, Mozambique had been a colonial vestige of Portugal in Africa, not allowed to, or quite incapable of making any decisions for herself. All eyes were traditionally turned to Mother Portugal, from whom all decisions for the future of the province were made.

Lack of political awareness, the restrictions on a free Press, and a simmering fear of the political police had left most people in Mozambique right outside politics and the military coup in Portugal left most confused, even bewildered, with their new-found freedom.

Just about everyone in Mozambique thought the April 25 coup and the military junta of General Antonio de Spinola that followed it was for the better, but nobody seemed to know why. It was all a bit confusing and minds strait-jacketed by 42 years of censorship withdrew from the mental challenge entirely or, in some cases, engaged themselves in wild and naive flights of political fantasy, notably in the capital of Lourenco Marques.

To put the coup in Portugal into perspective and to relate its significance to Mozambique and the delicate balance of power in Southern Africa, it might be useful briefly to look at Portugal's position just before the military takeover.

Pressure was beginning to mount on Dr Marcello Caetano's Government from almost every quarter.

Portugal had been fighting guerrilla wars in Africa for 13 years. Portugal had been fighting since 1961 in Guinea-Bissau, since 1963 in Angola and since 1964 in Mozambique when the first armed hostilities began in the territory. Thirteen years of debilitating war in Africa was taking its toll on Portugal.

The cost had been staggering. London's International Institute of Strategic Studies estimated that Portugal, at the time of writing, had spent more than two billion rands to finance her three wars in Africa. The heavy burden on the economy (Portugal was spending 43 per cent of her national budget on the war effort) ultimately was being carried by the taxpayer and the Portuguese were paying a 15 per cent "war tax" at home on many consumer goods.

Add to this the enormous psychological impact of young Portuguese men, crippled for life in the African wars, returning to Portugal and it is easy to see why political pressure was mounting in Portugal to find a solution to the African question.

Many of Portugal's young men didn't want to fight in the African provinces in any case. At the time of the coup, according to the Institute, 140 000 conscript soldiers from Portugal were holding up Portugal's tottering colonial ediface in Guinea-Bissau, Angola and Mozambique. In Mozambique there were 55 000. Rather than face two and a half years' conscription in Africa, young men were leaving

Portugal at the rate of 10 000 a year and no small country can afford to alienate its youth on that scale.

To take the situation in Mozambique, the White civilian population was also getting tired of the war and the toll it was taking on material and human resources in the province. Because of the domestic political pressure that was mounting in Portugal, fewer metropolitan troops were being sent to the province, and since 1968 the Mozambique army had undergone a localisation programme to recruit more locals for the army. Consequently, many people in Mozambique began thinking Portugal was relinquishing her responsibilities in the province.

This had a disturbing effect on Mozambique Whites, most of whom have no stake in Portugal. Their future is wrapped up in the future of Mozambique, and the seeds of fear were beginning to grow in their hearts. Many saw the war as being the only real solution to safeguard their future and they feared a Portuguese sellout in Mozambique, much like the French example in Algeria.

To the politically aware, it was becoming increasingly obvious that the war in Mozambique was really a revolutionary war and that Frelimo had outstripped the Portuguese in the battle for the hearts and minds of the local population.

The war in Mozambique was only 30 per cent military and 70 per cent psychological. The military's role was only to hold off Frelimo long enough to allow the civilian administration to develop the territory, meet the material aspirations of the local population and thus, at least theoretically, win the local people over to the benefits of Portuguese paternalism.

It did not take much analytical prowess to see that while the military was doing its job – indeed for 10 long years exceeding all expectations considering how poorly equipped it was – the civil arm was falling way behind and Frelimo was not waiting for them to catch up the backlog. Frelimo was converting minds to its cause much faster than the Portuguese – and a politically aware Black population in Mozambique would not have stood for what really amounts to Portuguese colonialism for much longer than it had to.

The seeds of an indigenous Black nationalism were beginning to emerge in Mozambique, hesitantly, but definitely there. The military knew it and reluctantly admitted it, but the civilian authorities denied it. They, too, must have read the signs clearly, but refused to admit it because it would have amounted to a tacit acknowledgement that they had not done their job.

This had led, in Mozambique at least, to a clear split between the military and civilian authorities, which was bound to come to a head sooner or later. For 10 years the military had learnt the hard way in Mozambique and in those 10 long years the military, and more especially the junior officers who had seen the realities in the field, had evolved definite ideas on how to terminate hostilities in the province, and they were not thinking of a military solution.

The big question was: could the civilian authorities, the politicians, who had lost touch with the realities of the situation, negotiate a peace? Could they even accommodate the thought of a political rather than a military solution to the war?

The answer to these questions came on April 25, when the Caetano Government was ousted by the Movement of the Armed Forces, led by conservative, but reformist junior officers – the men who were in touch with realities and had lost all confidence in the politicians in Portugal, in whose hands the future of the African provinces rested.

This, roughly, was the situation in Mozambique, but there was an even more delicate problem – the steadily declining support for Portugal's "last stand against Communism in Africa" among the Western powers, Portugal's traditional allies.

When the war in Mozambique started in 1964, Portugal drew her support from the member countries of the North Atlantic Treaty Organisation (NATO), Portugal being a member of NATO since 1949. Her original application for membership of the United Nations had been turned down because of the opposition of the Soviet Union, and it was only in 1955 that she was admitted.

Frelimo, on the other hand, drew its support from sympathisers in the United States and the Afro-Asian bloc.

In the East versus West ideological war the allignment of power shifted over the years. The USA, NATO and South Africa and Rhodesia supported Portugal and the Afro-Asians and the Communist bloc, Russia and China, supported Frelimo. With the assassination of Dr Eduardo Mondlane, the Western-oriented president of Frelimo, the organisation in 1969, finally linked arms with the Communists.

Portugal has always seen her African wars as an extension of East versus West and to see them in those terms – and the Mozambique war in particular may explain, at least in general terms, Portugal's "gentle revolution" of April 25, 1974, and why the hardline military junta that took control went "soft" on Socialism and Communism after the coup.

With each passing year of war, Portugal lost more of her already withering international support and was facing the almost inevitable prospect of total isolation, which would force her into an unhappy marriage with South Africa and Rhodesia and cut her off from Europe.

Already, besides her traditional enemies – Russia and China and the member countries of the Organisation of African Unity (OAU) – Western countries like Sweden, Denmark, Norway, Holland and India had turned against her. Even Britain, Portugal's oldest ally, an association dating back to the Treaty of Windsor in 1386, had turned hostile. Under a tottering Labour Government, returned to power in 1974, Britain would certainly be even more hostile since Prime Minister Harold Wilson is considered by many as an opportunist political animal who, for political advantage, would run with the hare and hunt with the hounds, a devious person whose peak in political oratory consists of personal attacks on his enemies. Known in Africa as the "Butcher of Biafra," history will put him into perspective by giving its late verdict.

Significant political pressure groups, notably influential Church groups in the USA and West Germany, Portugal's greatest ally in Europe, had also turned sour and were threatening to use their influence to break Portugal's fragile relationships with those countries.

The writing was on the wall for Portugal. As a Euro-African nation, with a foot in Africa and Europe, she was faced with a decision: to belong to Africa or Europe. She realised she could not sever ties with Europe, because geographically she was part of the Continent and, in any case, Europe was moving toward solidarity and economic cohesion through the European Economic Community (EEC).

The time had come for a massive political spring-clean in Portugal, something that would provide a possible solution to the wars in Africa; something that would remove the cobwebs that had gathered in the inner sanctums of government in Lisbon; and, finally, something that would make Portugal acceptable to Europe, which had moved considerably to the Left since World War II. It was necessary to gain the acceptance of Europe if she wanted to realign her traditional allies behind her in her avowed goal of keeping Africa open for the West and out of the hands of world Communism.

There were, as I see it, three options for Portugal before the military takeover: abandoning her African provinces; negotiating with the guerrilla movements in Africa; and continuing the wars.

Take the extreme option – to abandon her three African provinces and concentrate on Europe. This may not be as radical a solution as it seems. The French had opted for this solution in Algeria and President De Gaul came out of it as a statesman, for despite the anger it aroused among the Algerian French, an act of statesmanship it certainly was.

But this was an unlikely solution to Portugal's problems. Her whole economy was so interlinked with her African provinces that to abandon them would have had dire economic results and Portugal's historical fear of total dominance by her Iberian neighbour, Spain, could have become more than simply a nationalistic fancy.

Already the poorest country in Europe, Portugal without her African provinces, especially Angola which is the plum, would stand no chance in competition with her economically powerful West European neighbours.

Add to this the chauvinistic dream of 200-million Portuguese-speaking people around the globe, with the prospect of welding them into a transcontinental empire under some loose form of commonwealth and the option of abandoning her provinces in Africa was a bit more than the proud Portuguese spirit would allow. In any case, the Caetano Government was committed to the three wars in Africa and there seemed no likelihood of a change of policy.

There was also the possible political solution in negotiating with the guerrilla movements. Before the coup, however, Caetano's Government had stated unequivocally that it would not negotiate with the guerrillas. In Mozambique, the Portuguese Government refused even to accommodate the idea of negotiations with Frelimo because "Frelimo is representative of nobody in Mozambique". Frelimo, for its part, made an equal claim for the Portuguese, saying it would not negoitate with "any colonial or imperialistic" nation, and that meant Portugal.

Short of removing both stumbling blocks, a political solution of that nature seemed highly improbable.

There was also the option of fighting on into some distant and indeterminate future. For 10 years Portugal had fought her war in Mozambique on a shoestring and it was possible she could continue for at least another 10 years. This option was the least attractive. It would isolate Portugal in Europe, place an ever-increasing burden on her human and material resources, force her closer to White Southern Africa with its repugnant racial policies and would lead to an inevitable escalation in the war.

The prospect of a Southern African military bloc – embracing Angola, Mozambique, Rhodesia – and dominated by the militarily and economically powerful South Africa was not attractive to the Portuguese. Not only would Angola and Mozambique have to bear the brunt of the fighting, but they would inevitably fall more into the orbital influence of South Africa, which, in Portugal's avowed interest of creating non-racial enclaves in Africa, would be self-defeating. A racialist master was not Portugal's idea of her future in Africa, and fighting a war that could not be won was no solution either.

These basically were the options open to Portugal and none of them was particularly attractive nor capable of removing the insecurities facing Portugal in Africa and Europe.

Of these options, the Caetano Government had chosen the least attractive – to continue with the wars, presumably in the hope that one of her NATO allies would eventually come to her assistance.

Portugal had always hoped that the USA would provide aid for her African wars. Portugal has always been an enthusiastic member of NATO, which to her stands as the symbol of Western solidarity in the face of Communism. And Portugal has played her part by extending the courtesy of her Azores base in the Atlantic to the United States. The Azores agreement plays an important part in Portugal's relations with the USA. The use of the Azores is a vital part of the United States's global defence arrangements.

The Azores agreement was Portugal's trump card. The agreement terminated at the beginning of 1974 and at the time of writing had not been renegotiated. The Caetano Government, it appears, had hoped to use the Azores as its political bargaining power against the United States to try to get her to supply Portugal with arms for her African wars.

Thirteen years of war on the African continent, however, had un-

155

leashed a new political force, one that was to rock Portugal out of her "hawkish" attitude to her provinces in Africa and one that was to shake her out of her dilemma in Europe.

This new political force took the form of the Movement of the Armed Forces, the blossoming of the military into the political arena as a reaction to the instabilities of the present and insecurities of the future.

It was the catalyst needed to provide a possible solution to Portugal's manifold problems.

At core, the Movement of the Armed Forces was a spontaneous reaction to the bumblings of the politicians in Lisbon. A group of reformist junior officers, up to and including the rank of colonel, began to plot the overthrow of Caetano's Government which was ossifying in Europe.

They saw Portugal as having nothing to lose by a military takeover and everything to gain. If the movement failed, the politicians could bumble on in a similar fashion.

If it was successful, the least it could do would be to provide Portugal, committed to her stance in Africa, with a strong military government that was in touch with the realities of the situation in the African provinces.

Another reason for the coup in Portugal was rising concern in certain quarters that the allegations of Portuguese massacres in Mozambique were founded in fact.

The Times of London and a number of other Western newspapers published, late in 1973, allegations of massacres by Portuguese troops in the Tete district at Wiryamu and Chavola.

These reports were based on allegations made by Catholic missionaries in the area. The Portuguese Government denied the allegations, but the reports touched off an even greater introversion in the ranks of the Portuguese armed forces.

The allegations, at the time of writing, have not been proved beyond doubt and it is worth mentioning in passing that *The Times* of London acted irresponsibly in printing the allegations without substantiating them fully. It is interesting to note that London's *Daily Telegraph* handled the story with kid gloves as any responsible newspaper would in the circumstances and given the explosive nature of the allegations.

But regardless of the merits and morality of Fleet Street journalism, these reports alleging Portuguese massacres in Mozambique sparked off an investigation that took General Costa Gomes, the Portuguese Chief of Staff, to Nampula, the military headquarters of Mozambique, in February.

While he was there, he discussed the alleged massacres with Catholic clergy and with the Bishop of Nampula, Vieira Pinto.

There General Costa Gomes obtained evidence that a small minority of officers tolerated massacres and that they had been whitewashed by Right-wing officials.

Back in Portugal, General Costa Gomes agitated behind the scenes for a full inquiry into the massacre allegations and for reforms within the army to prevent future incidents that could stain Portugal's international image.

Another militating factor in the Movement of the Armed Forces was the publication of General Antonio de Spinola's politically explosive book, "Portugal and the Future".

Within three weeks the book had sold 50 000 copies and gone into new editions. It was a philosophical and political analysis of the nation's present and future and a suggestion for political and social development for her African provinces.

"We are able to arrive at the conclusion that, in any war of this type, an exclusively military victory is not viable," wrote the general.

What Spinola suggested was for the armed forces "to create and preserve for the necessary time – naturally not very long – the conditions of security that would allow social and political solutions, with an eye toward ending the conflict."

He wrote of the possibility of pulling out of Africa, but immediately rejected it because it would mean "abondaning loyal Portuguese". Therefore, the general wrote the choice was between a centralised system and a decentralised federal system. Largely because the three African provinces had different resources and different problems, Spinola opted for decentralisation, giving the overseas provinces wide powers to solve their own problems, but keeping defence, foreign affairs and finance in the hands of a simplified central Government in Lisbon.

"Must we remain in Africa?" wrote the general. "Yes. But not by armed might, nor by the subjugation of the Africans or by sustaining the myths the world paints about us. We must continue in Africa.

Yes. But with a clear vision of the problems in terms of a Portuguese solution."

Given the nature of the monocled general's support in the armed forces of Portugal and given the nature of the book's contents, a military takeover became a fait accompli.

But the Movement of the Armed Forces gained direct momentum without Spinola. Spinola, although having political aspirations, was a militarist and hardly a liberal and it would be hasty to conclude that he had anything to do with the coup besides indirectly adding to its momentum through his controversial book.

In December, 1973, 100 hardened combat captains signed a petition calling for reforms in the services. Spinola was immediately thought to be behind it. In fact, he was not. Nor did Spinola have a hand in the abortive coup in March of the following year which was crushed when DGS, the secret police, got wind of a planned march on the capital and thwarted the coup before it even got off the ground.

It was simply a matter of political bankruptcy. Spinola alone had emerged as the man most likely to be behind reformist moves. He was a creature of circumstance thrown into a role he had not expected to play.

Even on April 25, when the Movement of the Armed Forces finally ousted the Caetano Government, Spinola was an outsider. At 1,30 a.m. on the 25th he was approached to join the movement, but refused.

The rebel troops continued without Spinola. They entered Lisbon, and Prime Minister Caetano fled to the Carmo Barracks, headquarters of the regime's internal security troops, the National Republican Guard. There he waited for loyalist troops to counterattack. Very few did.

As the rebels stormed his sanctuary, Caetano asked to speak to Spinola, but the monocled general insisted he had no part in the coup and said he would only meet the Prime Minister if he had a mandate from the rebels, which he got immediately. And only then did Spinola take command.

Someone had to hold the reins and engineer the future direction of the coup and circumstances threw up the only man capable of the task. General Antonio de Spinola had waltzed into the history books without even trying, which is more than can be said for most politicians.

The Movement of the Armed Forces had ousted the old order and inadvertantly set the stage for one of the most sophisticated and ambitious political and diplomatic gambles in Portugal's long and chequered history.

It was G. K. Chesterton who wrote: "You can never have a revolution in order to establish a democracy. You must have a democracy to have a revolution". General Antonio de Spinola was intent on proving him wrong.

CHAPTER THIRTEEN

THE AFTERMATH IN PORTUGAL

Only two months after General Spinola had been fired from his position as Deputy Chairman of the nation's Joint Chiefs of Staff for advocating mild reforms in Portugal, he was the head of a "Junta of National Salvation" and the very future of Portugal lay at his feet. The world watched to see what decisions he would take.

Immediately he drew the most competent military leaders available around him. Besides himself, there were six other members of the junta: Naval Captain Antonio Alva Rosa Coutinho; Marine Captain Jose Baptista Pinho Azevedo; Brigadier Jaime Silverio Marques; Colonel Carlos Talvao de Melo; General Francisco da Costa Gomes (who had been fired two months earlier with Spinola) and the dashing Mozambique Air Force General Diogo Neto.

The seven-man military junta announced the country would return to civilian government and promised to institute reforms and the restoration of civil liberties. At the same time, the junta disbanded the old guard's National Popular Action Group, Portugal's only legal political party.

In a post-coup proclamation, the junta announced: "The Movement of the Armed Forces proclaims to the nation its intention to complete a programme of salvation for the country and the restitution to the Portuguese people of civil liberties of which they have been deprived."

The junta would be entrusted with the Government in the meantime. There would be general elections and the nation could freely choose its own form of social and political life.

Portugal had suddenly come of age and the promise of a better, less restricted future hung in the air. Political interest groups blossomed – 54 different groups rose out of the dust of 42 years of dictatorship – and it was a time for venting all the frustrations that had built up over generations.

But one thing was clear. Of the political groups that emerged immediately after the coup only two emerged as organised political parties: the Socialists and the Communists.

Four days after the coup, Socialist leader Mario Soares returned in triumph to Portugal from Paris where he had been living in exile.

Immediately after his return he issued a statement, saying: "We are ready to assume the highest responsibilities of office," and there was no doubt that the 49-year-old Socialist leader would do just that.

Soares was to play a key role in the post-coup arrangements. A lawyer and hard-core Socialist, Soares had been in exile since 1968 when he was defeated in the National Assembly elections. Exile was not new to him. He had been released from exile only a few months before the elections by former Prime Minister Caetano. The Socialist leader has a long history of controversy and imprisonment.

He was best known as the lawyer for the family of General Umberto Delgado, the Opposition leader, who once stood for President and who was found killed in Spain on April 24, 1965.

While attempting to leave Portugal on business in 1967, Soares was refused permission and a few months later arrested and imprisoned. He was released on March 1, 1968, and 18 days later he was rearrested and sent into exile on Sao Tome Island. It was his 12th arrest in 23 years. His first came when he was 21, for taking part in illegal workers' strikes. From then on, arrests, mostly on vague and unspecified charges, came with regularity.

In 1970, Soares outlined his thoughts on the Caetano regime and what he felt should be done with Portugal. They were surprisingly similar to what the military junta declared after the coup as its aims. The most important matter facing Portugal was the "colonial war on three fronts – Angola, Mozambique and Portuguese Guinea," he had said in the 1970 interview.

"It is a hopeless war which an underdeveloped country like Portugal could never be able to sustain without foreign aid.

"Should I come to power, I would at once enter into negotiations to stop the war. I recognise the principle of self-government and if those territories freely choose it, they should be independent," he said. Again, in 1972, Soares attacked the Portuguese Government on its policy in Africa. In June of that year his controversial book "Portugal Gagged," was seized by the Portuguese police. This book might have had a result as explosive as General Spinola's book, "Portugal and the Future", if it had not been impounded. Once again, in the book, Soares attacked Portugal on sensitive points, especially the African wars, which he called "wars without hope".

So when Soares returned to Portugal after the coup, he came with firm ideas for Portugal's future, closely resembling those of the military junta, but not exactly similar.

The junta's immediate message to the nation one day after the coup was simply: "The military junta guarantees the survival of the nation as a sovereign country in its multicontinental entirety." This statement was significant because it outlined in its most general terms Spinola's attitude to the African provinces – that even if they did choose independence, it would be in a loose federation with Portugal. Soares and the Portuguese Socialists were not really as close to the junta in their ideas as it might at first have seemed.

The other political group that arose after the coup with the standing of a highly organised political party was the Communists. Communist leader Alvaro Cunhal, who had also been in exile under the Caetano Government, also returned to Lisbon after the coup. Because the Communist Party had been forced underground in Portugal it had had to maintain rigid discipline and when, after the coup, the ban on the Communists was lifted by the military junta, the Portuguese Communist Party emerged as the most organised party in the country.

The Left-wing, then, emerged dominant after the coup, but the military were still in control. Given the conservative nature of the Movement of the Armed Forces, and indeed of General Spinola himself, it is interesting to speculate on the reasons why Spinola and his junta recalled the Socialists and Communists into the Political life of Portugal.

Spinola had adopted a slightly left-of-centre position on the political stage of Portugal. The time had come for negotiations at every level and this included the Left-wing, which, despite years of suppression, has considerable support in Portugal. Portugal has traditionally been in the grip of the "100 families", the rich landowners and wealthy industrialists, who virtually controlled the economy. Because of its wealth, this group represents a significant political pressure group in Portugal and it is rigidly conservative in outlook and oligarchic in nature.

Spinola's moderate centrist position allowed him to manoeuvre freely between the Socialists and Communists on the Left and the Democrats and moneyed interests to the Right. This was not through force of circumstances. Having gained power, Spinola's blueprint for the future of a multicontinental Portugal had to start in Metropolitan Portugal itself.

He had to try and rid Portugal of extremists on both sides of the political spectrum if he wanted to bring his plans to fruition. By accommodating the Socialists, Spinola could win back the support of the Socialist-oriented Western nations: Holland, Denmark, Sweden, Finland, Norway and Britain. By allowing Socialism its head in Portugal, it was feasible that Portugal would become acceptable to Europe, which since the Second World War has moved steadily toward Socialism more through force of circumstances than through any deep ideological conviction.

It was necessary for Portugal to realign her European allies if she wanted to share in the future of Europe. Spinola knew it, and it is probably for this reason that he recalled Mario Soares and eventually gave him the portfolio of Foreign Affairs in the provisional Government.

It may have been a condition laid down by Soares to return to Portugal and play his part in Portugal's future that Communist leader Alvaro Cunhal was also recalled. There was always the possibility of a later Socialist-Communist alliance for electoral purposes – much like in France – because European Communist parties although small in membership have always managed to command significant numbers of votes.

But another possible explanation for recalling the Communist leader was that Spinola felt it better to have the Communists out in the open where, under Spinola's new liberalisation policies, any active opposition from the Communists would discredit the party among the electorate.

Although banned under the Caetano regime, the Communists had been active in Portugal, particularly in the industrial suburbs of Lisbon. But due to strenuous persecution by the regime, the party was small. Two radical splinter groups linked with the party, LUAR and ARA, were responsible for a number of bomb attacks.

It seems reasonable to assume, however, that despite its dedication, the Communist Party's model would be too radical an alternative for Portugal, and Spinola was banking on the hard-core conservatism that runs through Portuguese society to isolate the Communists. It should be remembered that Caetano's gradual liberalising policies in Portugal had not been accepted lightly by the Right in Portugal and the threat of a Right-wing coup had hung in the air since the early days of Caetano.

The Communist Party leader, Alvaro Cunhal, eventually was appointed Minister without Portfolio in Spinola's provisional Government. To isolate the Communists by parliamentary means would surely convince her allies, notably the United States, that Portugal had not changed her attitude to Communism in any significant way, a move that would maintain Portugal's relationship with the United States and, indeed, strengthen it as the aspects of Portuguese policy under Caetano that were distasteful to America had been removed.

On the other extreme of the political spectrum, the Right-wing extremists in Portugal had become superfluous the moment the Movement of the Armed Forces decided there could be no military solution to Portugal's wars in Africa and by removing the Fascist elements in Portuguese society – notably the DGS and its fellow travellers – Portugal would be more acceptable to her European neighbours.

The elections promised by Spinola's military junta will be held in March, 1975. There seems a strong possiblity that in the period leading up to the elections the moderate conservative elements in Portugal will be able to group themselves in to a cohesive political party to fight the elections.

It is a challenge to the conservative elements of Portuguese society, which for 42 years have been complacent and it seems probable that they will rise to the challenge to meet the twin electoral attacks of the Socialists and Communists, who, in turn, might form an electoral alliance.

Spinola's blueprint for Portugal is a gamble, but a gamble that had to be taken. It only remains to be seen whether it will pay off. If it doesn't, Portugal will have jumped from the frying pan into the fire, and the dreams of a Portuguese empire will lie shattered on the history books.

If it pays off, Portugal will have taught the world that revolution can create a democracy and a progressive democracy at that, and General Antonio de Spinola will have emerged as one of the greatest statesmen of the decade.

The junta's first major setback came only 10 weeks after the provisional Government was established. The Prime Minister, Dr.

Adelino da Palma Carlos, and four Cabinet Ministers resigned their posts.

The 10-week-old Centre-Left coalition Government had floundered and the Prime Minister had quit because he said the State Council, Spinola's highest advisory body, refused to give the Prime Minister all the authority he requested.

But the real reason was the deep-seated split in the provisional Government between the Left and the Right in the Cabinet and the disagreement of members over the pace of decolonisation in Africa.

The conservatives, Communists, Socialists and liberals were finding it difficult to pull together and the leadership vacuum left in Portugal after nearly 50 years of dictatorship had made effective decision-making impossible.

Portugal was suddenly slipping dangerously toward economic chaos and political stalemate that threatened the very existence of the nation.

Spinola did the only possible thing. He fired the remainder of his Cabinet and appointed a military man, Colonel Vasco Goncalves, as Portugal's second post-coup Prime Minister.

The new 17-member Cabinet, appointed soon afterwards, had seven military men and a civilian coalition including Soares as Foreign Minister and Cunhal as Minister without Portfolio. The Socialist and Communist Parties once again had a foothold in the Government, but the Cabinet had a distinct military flavour.

The signs were clear. Spinola wanted order and the military were given a firm hold on the Presidency, the Cabinet and the influential State Council. The creation of a democracy from a dictatorship had not been simply a matter of ousting the dictator. Spinola had been forced, once again, to step in and put the political house in order and Portugal had taken a significant step to the Right. It may not be the last.

The stage is set for an interesting political battle in Metropolitan Portugal, but of far more interest is the future of Portugal's three African provinces, and Mozambique in particular.

CHAPTER FOURTEEN

THE AFTERMATH IN MOZAMBIQUE

News of the coup did not reach the capital of Mozambique, Lourenco Marques, immediately. It was a full day before the newspaper, *A Tribuna*, published a special edition giving details of developments in Portugal. Every edition of the paper was sold out in 30 minutes as enthusiastic crowds thronged the streets. The kerbside cafes were overflowing with jubilant citizens taking in the news. There had been rumours of a change in Portugal as far north as Nampula, but when the news broke only a select handful of people in Mozambique knew what actually had happened.

The rising excitement at the news and the political freedom it would inevitably bring to Mozambicans, however, was tainted with concern: what would happen to Mozambique now? Nobody really knew and many of Mozambique's 250 000 Whites began to realise that life for them perhaps would never be the same again.

The immediate effects of the coup were the firing of the Governor General of Mozambique, Mr Pimentel dos Santos, and Mozambique's nine district governors.

The orders to the Governor General to quit came in the form of a cable from the military junta in Lisbon. It must have come as a shock to him because he clung to power until the last, issuing statements that he was still officially and legally in command of the territory. But the die was cast and he relinquished office.

At the same time, the military junta downgraded the powerful secret police, DGS, and relegated them to an intelligence wing of the army. But DGS atrocities soon became known, and DGS agents were either rounded up and imprisoned or hounded out of Mozambique, some to seek a refuge in South Africa and Rhodesia, others to "disappear" farther afield. Hundreds of political prisoners were released from Lourenco Marques's Machava jail, where it was claimed DGS agents had tortured inmates and allegedly buried some of them alive.

Like their counterparts in Portugal, Mozambicans had a new-found freedom and it went to their heads.

I had returned to Mozambique in the interim to watch developments there, and from Lourenco Marques in the south to Nampula in the north people were watching and waiting, all eyes turned to Lisbon as they awaited news of the junta's future plans for the province.

Most interest was centred around the capital, Lourenco Marques, where within two weeks of the coup 52 political groups emerged, issuing proclamations and holding public meetings to get their political ideas across to the residents and the world in general. Some of the meetings were unruly as different interest groups vied for a platform. It all led to a colossal confusion out of which emerged only two parties that appeared to have widespread support and which could have become political forces in the new Mozambique.

One was GUMO (Group for Unification of Mozambique). One of the leading lights in this moderate multi-racial organisation was Mrs Joanna Simeao, whose charisma immediately grabbed the interest of many residents and of the international Press and television that had converged on the capital.

I met Mrs Simeao in her neat downtown apartment a few weeks after the coup. GUMO, by that stage, had established itself as one of the leading political parties in Lourenco Marques. It had been the first to emerge after the coup and its initial impact was considerable.

Mrs Simeao, wearing gold-rimmed spectacles, a multi-coloured turban and a neat Swazi-type caftan, told me what her organisation stood for.

"We want a peaceful solution for Mozambique. We believe the only way to end the violence is through negotiation with Frelimo. But Mozambique must also have its independence," she said.

Mrs Simeao used to belong to Coremo, the guerrilla movement operating out of Zambia. Because of her activities, she was arrested and briefly imprisoned in Portugal. On her release, she went to Paris before returning to Mozambique where at the time she was teaching French.

GUMO was the most moderate of the groups that emerged in Lourenco Marques and was the most active after the coup. But GUMO meetings were also the most rowdy. In Lourenco Marques and in Beira, Gumo meetings were broken up. In Lourenco Marques, the Gumo meeting, addressed by Mrs Simeao, turned ugly when a large group of Blacks began shouting their support for Frelimo, and in Beira a Gumo meeting erupted into violence for a similar reason.

In that city there had been a Right-wing White backlash to the coup and the Black Frelimo supporters soon found themselves faced with an angry group of White residents.

Mrs Simeao, however, was expelled from GUMO a month later. The moderate organisation, at the time of writing, appears to have been swallowed up by the more extreme elements on both sides of the political spectrum. It appears the moderate approach to independence in Mozambique could not mobilise enough support in the current political climate to present a viable solution to Mozambique's shaky future.

The second significant political group to emerge from the sloganising was a group calling itself FICO, which means "I stay" or "remain" in Portuguese. The label FICO is formed from the initial letters of its full title "Independent Group for Retaining Ties with the West".

Membership of FICO was drawn from veterans of the 10-year war, and the White middle and working classes.

It first showed itself in Lourenco Marques when, in an emotional display, about 6 000 Fico members pledged themselves to continue the war with Frelimo and to the Portuguese flag. It was through Fico that the fears of Mozambique's silent White majority made itself heard.

It was from this phalanx of Right-wing Whites that the possibility of a Unilateral Declaration of Independence for Mozambique first arose. Many Whites I spoke to in the weeks after the coup were stung, many indignant, that Portugal wanted negotiations. They saw this as a tacit acceptance of defeat in Mozambique and the possibility of Black majority rule, and a heavy Frelimo influence in Mozambique was repugnant to them. They had fought against that very possibility for 10 long years.

It was not surprising, then, that groups of unidentified Whites on the Right resorted to violence in Lourenco Marques and Beira, and rumours floated about that a White mercenary army was being established by Mike Hoare in Malawi to fight Frelimo and restore order in Mozambique. "Mad Mike", as he was tagged in the Congo where his mercenaries last fought, denied any involvement.

But none of the political groups that emerged in those early weeks in Mozambique took account of Frelimo itself. It would be naive to think that Frelimo did not have considerable grassroot support in

Mozambique at the time of the coup and it seemed inevitable that this would make itself felt.

The real political force in Mozambique, Frelimo, was waiting and watching. The military junta had announced that there would be no Portuguese sellout in Mozambique. General Spinola had made it clear that if the African provinces wanted "outright independence" Portugal would not accommodate them. Spinola's answer was still a gradual move toward self-determination under the maternal wing of Portugal and retaining links with Portugal once independence was attained.

It was obvious Frelimo was letting the steam cool off in Mozambique, waiting in the background to see what would develop. In the meantime, Frelimo continued its attacks; in fact, intensified them in the weeks just after the coup, and in Dar es Salaam, in Tanzania, the president of Frelimo, Samora Machel, repeatedly stated Frelimo would not negotiate with Portugal, though there seemed little doubt Frelimo would meet Portuguese envoys to have Portugal's position clarified before making any final decisihns on its future direction in Mozambique.

In fact, it did, and although talks broke down and negotiators decided to meet "in camera", it was clear Frelimo would speak to the Portuguese, but only on its own terms -- immediate independence.

I had been in the north of Mozambique, in Nampula, sounding out sources close to the army and getting the feel of the local population. In Nampula it was as if nothing had changed. But it had, and the White residents were anxious. The No. 2 man of the military junta in Portugal, General Costa Gomes, was due to arrive in Mozambique the following week to spell out Mozambique's future, and Nampula, as indeed all of Mozambique, awaited his arrival with a mixture of excitement and trepidation.

Back in Lourenco Marques, with a large group of international journalists, I waited for General Gomes's arrival. Only the previous week I had stood at the same airport terminal to see the departure of Admiral of the Navy Moura Da Fonseca, who had been sacked by the junta and recalled to Portugal. I felt extremely sorry for him as he said goodbye to a small group of naval officers and friends. He had been stripped of his rank and left Mozambique as a civilian.

He looked shaken and, although he retained his dignity, he seemed to have shrunk since last I saw him – trousers rolled up to the knee as he waded out to his boat at Palma, in Cabo Delgado.

We shook hands and I asked him why he had been recalled.

"I don't know. I am not at odds with the junta, but I have been told to return to Portugal," he said.

"I'm sorry."

"Yes. Thank you." And with those brief words he moved into the VIP lounge where he sat waiting for the plane that would take him back to Lisbon.

In the weeks that followed the coup, there were many grey-faced senior officers in Mozambique. A cable from Portugal was enough to shatter a career and a lifetime of dreams, so it was not surprising to see anxiety etched on the faces of many of the officers who, a week later, stood waiting at the airport to greet General Costa Gomes.

The large crowd clapped as the General, accompanied by Air Force General Diogo Neto, who had become the No. 3 man in the junta, arrived.

He made a brief statement and was wisked off in a motor cavalcade to the Governor's palace where he was to hold a Press conference the next afternoon.

General Costa Gomes's Press conference was chaotic. But what emerged was an offer to Frelimo to come into Mozambique as a bona fide political party and fight in an open election. The General said there was only one proviso; that Frelimo cease fighting. It occurred to me that this was a somewhat weaker statement than that made by Spinola after the coup. General Costa Gomes said that if Frelimo did not accept Portugal's offer, Portugal would have no option but to continue the war and escalate it with her full military capability which given the circumstances seemed like a rather hollow threat.

And that was how things stood when I left Mozambique for the second time in four months. The future of Mozambique certainly had not been spelt out by General Costa Gomes. He had offered the war-torn province a possible alternative to war.

It would be rash to attempt to foresee what will happen in Mozambique. There is such a multiplicity of existing and potential variable operating in the territory that any prognosis is a very tentative exercise.

Initially Frelimo was faced with the choice of fighting on or negotiating with Portugal. At the time I could only speculate on those two options and how each could affect Mozambique.

The first option – to continue fighting – was always possible. The intensification of Frelimo attacks after the junta's peace proposals was seen by many observers as a move by Frelimo to increase its bargaining power once it did come to the conference table. Frelimo, it was thought, would be in a stronger negotiating position if it had increased its military effort before a peace conference.

It was significant to notice China's reaction to the coup in Portugal. China made it clear her attitude would hinge on how the colonial issue was handled. Generally, China's argument was that the people of Mozambique "had not shed so much of their blood to submit to neo-colonialism". China had refused to open diplomatic relations with South Africa, Rhodesia, Israel and Portugal (the only European nation not recognised by China) because of those countries' colonial policies.

China's influence in Frelimo did not suddenly cease because of the coup in Portugal. A political solution to the war in Mozambique would not have been in China's interests.

In the second colonial race, China has not been slow in taking the lead in Africa. Africa is the last untapped continent and China, like Russia, wants a stake in it. The former European colonial powers have retained their stake through neo-colonialism . . . economic dominance by the former colonial power. China and Russia, not being in the first scramble for Africa, are certainly pioneering the second. China's interests in Southern and Central Africa would not have been served by the cessation of hostilities in Mozambique.

As long as Frelimo continued fighting, Chinese interests were served because it gave her more time to entrench herself, which she had shown herself to be adept at doing in the 10 years of fighting in Mozambique. With each passing year of war, Frelimo necessarily became more indebted to China. It would be naive to think that China's contributions to Southern African liberation movements was for egalitarian reasons, and the depressing prospect remains that her motives are to entrench herself on the African continent – no more, no less.

By pressurising Frelimo to continue with its struggle, China would have been working toward an escalation of the war. Portugal already strained to the limit would have been hard pressed to continue going it alone in Africa and the prospect of American or even West European involvement could turn Mozambique into a second Vietnam.

Significant in this respect was the warning given by the influential American Security Council, a Right-wing, private organisation based in Washington with close links with the Pentagon.

A recent paper issued by the council states: "Frelimo uses Soviet equipment and they have considerable debts to their suppliers. The door is wide open for the Soviets and the Chinese to step in. If Mozambique falls to Frelimo, the Communists will have bases from which to attack South Africa." And, it continues, America would not stand idly by if Communist action threatened South Africa.

It would have been a sound measure of Chinese influence in Frelimo if it had continued the struggle. According to the Frelimo constitution, one of the main aims of Frelimo is: "The defence and realisation of all aspirations of all the people of Mozambique, exploited and oppressed by the Portuguese colonial regime."

If Frelimo did not negotiate with Portugal and try to gain total independence for Mozambique it would have been assumed that China's influence was greater in the movement than most observers thought.

CHAPTER FIFTEEN

MOZAMBIQUE AND THE WHITE SOUTH

White Southern Africa is at the crossroads. Developments in Mozambique must surely provide a salutory lesson to Rhodesia and South Africa: that they must come to terms with their Black populations while the climate is still right for negotiating an equable future for all their racial groups.

The much-quoted "domino theory" – that the "fall" of Mozambique will necessarily lead to the "fall" of the White, Western-oriented governments of Rhodesia and South Africa does not necessarily follow, but judged on the events in Mozambique it does follow that Rhodesia and South Africa are going to have to do some serious rethinking if they are to avoid long-term military confrontations with Black nationalism, which, unfortunately, has naively linked arms with international Communism in Southern Africa.

Judged on the modern examples of guerrilla war, Rhodesia and South Africa must also recognise the dangers of getting involved in a guerrilla war. Rhodesians and South Africans are probably better mentally equipped than most to fight this type of war, but unless they can rely on the full support of their Black people, the prospect of winning a war of this nature is small. Can Rhodesia and South Africa rely totally on their Black people? Based on the history of race relations in those two countries, the answer cannot be an unequivocal "yes".

Rhodesia is in a particularly precarious position. White Rhodesia was founded by force and for eighty years has successfully maintained itself by economic and military superiority. Faced with the undaunting White supremist attitudes of Rhodesia's 230 000 Whites, the militant nationalist section of the Black population has already resorted to guerrilla tactics in Rhodesia's north-eastern district. Although this may only be a natural reaction to the political consciousness that followed the post-UDI conflict with Britain and may be shortlived, it is more likely that the current guerrilla activity in Rhodesia is only the start of a long and debilitating war, which the Rhodesian security forces cannot and will not win alone.

Since Rhodesia declared UDI in November, 1965, it has addressed itself to the symptoms of Black discontent rather than to underlying causes and the Rhodesian Front Government of Mr Ian Smith has shown no indication that it will change its attitudes.

It would seem that Rhodesia is on a collision course with Black nationalism. In contrast to South Africa, it is unlikely that Rhodesia can muster the resources, both human and material, to maintain a long-term guerrilla struggle.

Nor can Rhodesia look for overt assistance from South Africa. South Africa's international position is precarious enough without having to take on the international storm that would follow in the wake of South African involvement in Rhodesia. It would seem more likely that South Africa would continue to give under-the-table support for the Smith Government, using Rhodesia in the same way it used Mozambique – as a buffer State.

But rather than risk uncontrolled conflict in Rhodesia, South Africa would probably work toward the controlled implementation of majority rule in Rhodesia. A Black-majority Government in Rhodesia would be much like those in Malawi, Swaziland, Botswana and Lesotho, which are satellite nations in the economic orbit of South Africa. While paying lip-service to the Organisation of African Unity (OAU), these countries must for their own economic survival retain good relations with South Africa.

It is interesting to look at remarks made by the Rhodesian Prime Minister in an interview with William Buckley, a well-known conservative American television interviewer, just before the coup in Portugal.

"Haven't you been having a certain amount of trouble along the Mozambique frontier and, if so, why is it that the Portuguese aren't in a position to patrol successfully and prevent the terrorists from launching attacks from Mozambique?" asked Buckley.

This was Mr Smith's answer: "I regret to say this is something I am unable to explain. The terrorists have been gaining ground in Mozambique. I think it is the hope of the people in Mozambique that eventually they will get on top of this. They are embarking on certain policies. It is a fact, I believe, that the completion of the Cabora Bassa Dam will provide a certain amount of assistance and we are hopeful that the position will improve, but at the moment this is one of our weak points. We have been fairly successful in holding the line on the Zambesi. Apart from sporadic hit-and-run raids, we now find that these people have come around and through Mozambique and they caught us unawares there. And this has taken us a little longer than we anticipated. I am completely confident that we will get on top of the problem and solve it."

That was exactly one month before the coup in Portugal, and Portugal's decision to extend the hand of friendship to Frelimo must have undermined Mr Smith's rather naive confidence.

Mr Smith's intelligence on the position in Mozambique must either have been optimistic or Mr Smith was trying to allay the fears of his white electorate, something he has shown himself to be quite adept at doing.

Mr Smith had obviously taken the Portuguese presence too much for granted, just as he appears to take the patience of his Black majority too much for granted.

Rhodesia in the early 1950s – during the period of Federation with Northern Rhodesia (Zambia) and Nyasaland (Malawi) – had introduced a number of reforms, which pointed to a change from the earlier colonial type of White supremacy to a limited and contrived racial competition. Racial policy in Rhodesia was changed in midstream. African trade unions were accepted in 1954 as being necessary and two years later an amendment to the Industrial Conciliation Act was made to include Africans in the definition of employee. African education was speeded up, African agricultural competition was encouraged and Government appropriations for African agriculture increased roughly eightfold in the 1950s.

At the same time, an African middle class was being fostered and reforms were engendered in the electoral system to enfranchise this class. Rhodesia seemed set on the path of compromise and evolutionary change.

But this period of reform and economic stabilisation failed dismally. The Constitution of December 6, 1961, provided for 65 seats in the Rhodesian Legislature, including 15 seats for Africans, who previously had none. The elections were held in December, 1962, and the Rhodesian Front, led by Winston Field won 35 seats. The ruling United Federal Party, led by Sir Edgar Whitehead, which had instituted the reforms won 29 seats. These constituencies returned 14 Whites, 14 Africans and one Coloured candidate. The Rhodesian Front formed a Government under the Premiership of Field; who resigned in April, 1964, in favour of Ian Smith.

175

In some ways it was not surprising that the Rhodesian Front came to power. The electorate had been stung by stories of the atrocities in the Congo and the rising dominance of Black nationalism to the north and the fear of domestic Black extremism. The success of the Rhodesian Front can largely be seen as an attempt to halt the wave of reforms during the federal period and more specifically to halt the process of constitutional advancement toward majority rule that went with them.

For the moment, the candle of Black nationalism had been extinguished and Rhodesia had returned to the White supremist ideology of the pre-Federal days. With the power switch to the Rhodesian Front, came the dissolution of the Federation, in 1963. The ensuing move toward independence was on, a move that led to UDI in November, 1965.

The Smith Government ostensibly had nipped Black nationalism in Rhodesia in the bud. But had it really? It would seem hard to believe that once the Black population's political aspirations had been boosted during the reform period under the Federation, that it would cease to exist with the return to White supremist ideology under the Rhodesian Front. It fact, it had not, and the emergence of guerrilla activities in Rhodesia in the 1970s bears witness to the fact that Black nationalism is alive and robust in Rhodesia.

Now the Portuguese have realised that Mozambique could not be held by military means and that Black majority rule was inevitable, Rhodesia is in a difficult position. It must decide to compromise or involve itself in an escalating guerrilla war. There seems little doubt that the guerrilla movements in Southern Africa will view the Portuguese call for negotiations as a victory for Black nationalism which could well spur on the anti-Rhodesian guerrilla movements to greater efforts.

White Rhodesia is in much the same position now as Mozambique was 10 years ago. But 10 years ago the minor irritant of guerrilla infiltrations into the north of Mozambique had little impact on Portuguese thinking. The Portuguese even believed they could rid themselves of terrorism by fighting it on its own terms. They were proved wrong.

Rhodesia is faced with a similar situation. Ten years ago the Portuguese would never have dreamed of negotiating with Frelimo. Today they have been forced to. Will Rhodesia learn from the

long corridors as the many newsmen gathered there tried to get their versions of the situation on the line first and to guard their news secrets.

It became a bit oppressive. At the time, I had teamed up with an old friend and newspaper colleague, Michael McCann, who was shooting pictures for *Time* magazine. Mike is based in Johannesburg, and to my mind is one of the most artistic news photographers in Africa.

We decided to spend the night on the town, to get away from the incessant haste and urgency of the journalistic circle at the hotel. It turned out to be a memorable night.

Mike is a rather inscrutable person, a combination of romantic and pragmatist. Our talks together were never about our respective assignments, the war, or the political future of Mozambique. Instead we talked about building yachts and sailing off into the blue, cycling around Spain and generally about the idealistic notions of escapism that hold a particular excitement to all men at some time or another.

It was a good way to relax from the realities of the past few weeks and the war in Mozambique could never have been more distant.

After a refreshing meal we walked down some unnamed street on our way back to the hotel until we came across a small restaurant well removed from the street and illuminated by a dull blue glare that glowed through the frosted transom above the door facing the pavement.

It was already quite late, but Lourenco Marques was just coming alive. Black and green taxi cabs rushed past in a seemingly endless flow to the city centre where the neon lights would be flickering and inviting people to savour the life offered inside. Night clubs, strip joints, bars filled with women and the catching excitements of streetwalkers who have long lost all inhibitions to ply their trade on lonely visitors.

A gentle breeze was playing off the bay, curving the giant palm trees across the road and flicking little bits of salty spray around the darkened suburbs.

We entered the restaurant and found ourselves sitting at the back among a small group of Portuguese diners. The lights were dim and the wine was extremely good. At the head of the small restaurant was an open space where two burly Portuguese men were tuning their instruments in preparation for a fado, the traditional Portuguese song that has been so aptly described as "the soul of Portugal".

Grouped in couples or sitting alone, the diners took it all in: the dim lighting, the heavy wines and always the music – haunting, sad, reflexive – dreams of better times, happier days.

We sat listening to the plaintive songs as they echoed through the room and seemed to fill the place with a heavy melancholy. The diners listened, joined in at times and filled themselves with the sad intonations of the singer's voice. Once again the inherent sadness of the Portuguese nation was brought home to me as the music filtered around me building little sorrows in the heart's labyrinthine turnings.

Then a man and a woman entered. She was one of the most striking women I have seen, a combination of Moor and metropole: shining blue-black hair caught behind in a tight bun. She held her head up with the condescending arrogance of an aristocrat, yet she was totally feminine, the type of woman who should be put on a pedestal there to gloat at the world of lesser beings and mock the middle-class pretentions of the "liberated" woman. She wore black, and the effect of her jet black hair and her Victorian clothing brought her face out in stark relief, like the chiaroscuro effect of a Rembrandt painting.

She walked the length of the room and sat down. I was captivated by her. She seemed to have brought the fado into its perspective, the living personification of what the music was trying to evoke.

The evening wore on. All the tourists had left and we were the last visitors in the restaurant. The owner walked over to us, gave us a second bottle of wine gratis and told us in a haughty way, but not without enthusiasm, that we were privileged as that evening all the guests remaining were part of a "family of fado singers".

True to his word the remaining guests formed a circle and began to sing the fado, each in turn standing and singing from the heart.

It came to the turn of the lady dressed in black. She stood up, head held high, hands clasped in front of her Junoesque body, and began to sing.

Her voice had the mellow, endearing ring of a trained contralto. She began very softly, the notes hanging on her lips like heavy memories of the past. As she progressed through the song, her body began to weave backwards and forwards, forcing each forward note out with a studied jerk of her head. She built up to a climax, her rich voice filling the entire room with a sound that trickled down my spine and had me on my feet applauding as the final note broke the heavy air.

She opened her eyes, bringing her thoughts back from the cobbled streets of "Lisboa" where she had been wandering, searching for her lover, and turned to face me as I stood clapping in my dark corner. A faint smile played across her lips, and for a brief, discreet moment her black eyes flashed across the room, piercing me at a distance.

She bowed her head slightly, then nodded to the players to strike up another song. Ignoring the other company, she turned to face me and began singing, this time her body quivering with emotion, totally given to the song. Her flashing eyes held mine through the song. It was a moment of complete communication, everything that could ever be said was said in that song.

In those moments everything I had done in Mozambique over the past few weeks suddenly became irrelevant, distant murmers from a hazy past, a past that had already been swallowed up by the future. She was the only constant; then and there forcing all notions of time and space into the wings of my consciousness. It was a total escape.

When we left at 3 a.m., Mike and I to our lonely hotel rooms and she with her husband to some unseen block of flats or suburban house on the fringes of Lourenco Marques, we still had not spoken to each other and yet we had walked away into our respective darknesses with a new understanding.

It was one of life's simplest messages: that communication comes not through words, promises, treaties or wars, but through a little human understanding, something that the war-torn province of Mozambique is going to have to find a lot of in the ensuing months of its new-found freedom.

183

POSTSCRIPT

With recent events, it looked as though Mozambique's immediate political future would be assured.

More than 400 years of Portuguese rule in the territory came to an end – "officially" – on Friday, September 6, 1974, when an agreement was reached on the independence of this war-torn Portuguese province.

The agreement was signed by Dr. Mario Soares, the Socialist Portuguese Foreign Minister, and Samora Machel, the president of Frelimo.

The agreement gave Frelimo self-governing powers from September 25. The struggle for this lonely outpost of Portugal in Africa is over – "officially" – and it seemed the swords were sheathed and only the mental scars remained. But who knows what the future really holds?

The scars of the 10-year guerilla struggle, however, are grievous. For 10 years thousands of men from Portugal and Mozambique fought a war against "terrorist" – or "freedom" – forces who were dedicated to the destruction of Portugal in Africa. Not all of them believed in the struggle.

To many of these men it was a call to duty, a patriotic gesture to Portugal and the dream of a Lusitanian community. Many died; many were maimed and broken for that dream.

At the stroke of a pen that gesture became meaningless.

The enemy was to be accepted as the legitimate instrument of government in Mozambique, and metropolitan Portugal could hold its head up in the international community with impunity. The men who gave themselves to the struggle – many never to be seen again except as names in epitaphs in this obscure country on the east flank of Africa – were now just an appendage of history, forgotten soldiers in a forgotten war.

It is not surprising, therefore, that many of these men and the men who had made their mark on Mozambique's economy reacted strongly to Portugal's political act. It was not surprising that they drew the conclusion that their struggle had been wasted, that Portugal had sold them down the river; coldly and cynically.

It was also not surprising that as a gesture of defiance they took up arms once again, marched on the capital, Lourenco Marques, and declared a Unilateral Declaration of Independence. It was the only possible way of recovering some of their pride.

In the inevitability of majority rule it was a futile gesture in the circumstances, but a gesture that could not be lost on the politicians in Portugal for whom the circumstances might be regrettable, but irreversible nevertheless.

It is these men, right or wrong though the might be, who also deserve to be remembered.

Although Mozambique is set for independence, its struggle is just beginning. The new Government is faced with a number of decisions, decisions that can no longer be clouded in revolutionary rhetoric and propaganda. Old enemies have now to reconcile themselves to the fact that, unless they can find some mutual ground, Mozambique will erupt into a bloody battlefield of racial and tribal hostilities.

Those in charge have to build an administration that can develop the territory's resources to the benefit of all Mozambicans and run the country efficiently. They have to legitimise their new power and seek consensus in a plural society. Without these, the past bloodshed will become a permanent feature – a legacy of political stupidity.

But the greatest decision facing the new leaders is the relationship of Mozambique with South Africa. This should be the key decision: whether to sever all ties with its White supremist neighbour for ideological reasons, or whether to take the pragmatic line and receive the economic benefits that the old Mozambique derived from the South African economy.

This decision is crucial. It will affect many thousands of Mozambicans as South Africa provides Mozambique with 75 per cent of its foreign exchange. It is time for cool economic appraisal and political responsibility.

Development and modernisation are the real struggle, and the new politics is that of choice. The world now watches to see what choice is to be made. The key word is no longer *revolution*, but *responsibility*.

ORGANISATION OF FRELIMO DEFENCE DEPARTMENT

COMMANDER-IN-CHIEF
Samora Machel

DEPUTY

DISCIPLINARY COMMITTEE

SECTIONS

PERSONNEL

RECRUITMENT
INSTRUCTION AND
FORMATION OF
CADRES

RECCONAISSANCE

SECURITY

OPERATIONS

MATERIAL AND
TRANSPORT

INFORMATION AND
PROPAGANDA

POLITICAL
COMMISSARIAT

COMMUNICATION
AND LIAISON

HEALTH

ADMINISTRATION
FINANCE

SUB SECTIONS

ORGANISATION OF
THE MASSES

ADMINISTRATION

PRODUCTION
CO-OPS AND
COMMERCE

SOCIAL
AFFAIRS

GUERRILLA BASE CAMPS

TANZANIA

MBEYA – Frelimo office and stores – important stores for transit materials.

ARUSHA – Training camps of Tanzanian Army and Guerrillas. Only place where Russian instructors are used.

BAGAMOYO – Frelimo Education Centre – Secondary School only.

DAR-ES-SALAAM – Diplomatic and Political capital of Frelimo. Also houses "Mozambique Institute", Frelimo Education Centre for pre-university level.

NASHINGWEA – Military Capital: Command and Logistic Organisation. Also Frelimo training camp – Chinese instructors.

MTWARA – Frelimo office and stores. Only Frelimo hospital.

MHIAMBWE ⎫ –
MKUNIA ⎬ – Stores. Support and control of infiltration into
SINDANO ⎭ – Cabo Delgado.

TUNDURU – Education centre. Capital of Frelimo Education Department.

SONGEA – Frelimo office and headquarters for Niassa district.

BILANDJE ⎫
N'COLEZE ⎬ – Stores. Support and control of infiltration into
MITOMOUI ⎭ – Niassa.

ZAMBIA

SINDE MISSALE ⎫
TCHADIZA ⎪
KATHUMBA ⎬ – Stores. Support and control of infiltration
CASSUENDE ⎪ – into Tete.
MWANYA-WANTHU ⎪
CACHOLOLA ⎭

MACHEKA – Coremo base camp.

LUSAKA – Headquarters of Centre for Liberation of Africa.

FRELIMO STRUCTURE AT A SUPERIOR LEVEL

CONGRESS	Every 2 years

CENTRAL COMMITTEE	PRESIDENT VICE-PRESIDENT DEPARTMENT HEADS PROVINCIAL SECRETARIES

POLITICAL AND MILITARY COMMITTEES	COMMISSIONS OF EXPERTS ON ALL ASPECTS OF FRELIMO AFFAIRS

EXECUTIVE COMMITTEE

PRESIDENT'S COUNCIL

DEPARTMENTS

DEFENCE
SECURITY
EXTERNAL AFFAIRS
INFORMATION AND PROPAGANDA
EDUCATION AND CULTURE
TREASUARY FINANCE AND COMMERCE

MOZAMBIQUE LIBERATION MOVEMENTS

I am deeply indebted to Mr Neil Bruce, who provided most of the following information in his excellent paper on Portugal's wars in Africa, published by Conflict Studies, London.

1. *African National Association of the Moatize*—Anam. Created in 1959 in Tete District, to subvert the people of this economically important Moatize coal-producing region. Transformed into *União Africana de Moçambique Independente*—African National Union for the Independence of Mozambique—Unami.

2. *Mozambique African Nationalist Union*—Manu. Founded in 1960 in Tanganyika to unite the Maconde tribesmen in Tanganyika. Existed later only as a pressure group *inside* Tanganyika, but important because it *began* the insurrection and subversion in the Cabo Delgado district in August, 1964.

3. *União Democráçica Nacional de Moçambique*—National Democratic Union of Mozambique—Udenamo. Founded in Bulawayo, S. Rhodesia, in 1962, (by *Adelino Gwambe*, a contender for the leadership of Frelimo after the assassination of Dr Mondlane, as a result of personal rivalries and his expulsion from Frelimo). Fades out quickly, but reappears later. (See 5 below.)

4. *Frente de Libertação de Moçambique*—Mozambique Liberation Front—Frelimo. Formed 1962 to unify Unami, Manu and Udenamo.
Leader: Until his assassination at his headquarters in Dar es Salaam in February, 1969, Dr Eduardo Mondlane was the undisputed leader. After a prolonged struggle for leadership, *Samora Moyse Machel* elected head in May, 1970, and remains in this position. A former male nurse from Lourenço Marques, Samora Machel is a hard-line Communist, trained in Algeria and the USSR, though his organisation is dominated by Maoist cadres. Its arms come from Russia and Eastern European countries as well as China.
Headquarters: Dar es Salaam, Tanzania.
Training Centre and main operational centre: Nachingwea, in southern Tanzania. Frelimo remains the only valid guerrilla organisation in Mozambique recognised as such by the OAU.

5. *União Democrácica Nacional de Monomatapa*— Udenamo-Monomatapa. Founded by Adelino Gwambe in mid-1962, as a result of his failure to be elected president of Frelimo, and his eventual expulsion from that organisation. He reconstituted the old Udenamo, with the addition of the name of the leader of a great African Mozambique empire of the past, led by Muene Moutapa, or, in Portuguese, Monomatapa. It never really got off the ground, but this was by no means the end of Adelino Gwambe. (See 7, 8 and 9 below.)

6. *Kilimane Freedom Party* (Kilidom Party for Freedom). Formed at the end of 1962 in Salisbury, Rhodesia, together with Africans from Mozambique who lived or worked there. Later transformed into Manu - *Mozambique African National Congress.*

7. *Frente Unida Anti-Imperialista Popular Africana de Moçambique* - Popular United Anti-Imperialist Front for Mozambique - Funipamo. An attempt by *Adelino Gwambe* to unify Udenamo and Manu, and former adherents of Frelimo, into a new party based in Malawi. Little success.

8. *Comité Revolucionário de Moçambique* - Revolutionary Committee for Mozambique - Coremo. Formed soon after Zambian independence in 1964 by *Paulo Gumane*, this was an attempt to unite all anti-Portuguese organisations with interests in Mozambique. Unami and Manu (the opposition elements to Frelimo) joined. Frelimo withdrew. So ultimately Coremo was formed from Udenamo and Manu (*Adelino Gwambe*, president). Later in the year *Gwambe* was expelled.

It still has a base in Zambia; is Maoist-oriented; has a base camp in Zambia at *Macheke*, but suffers from the bitter opposition of Frelimo, as well as its smallness.

9. Movement for the Liberation of Mozambique - Molimo. Formed in mid-1970 as a splinter group of Frelimo. This movement is based in Nairobi, Kenya, and is led by Almeida Magaia. It is Maoist-oriented.

10. *Partido Popular de Monomatapa*—Popular Party of Mozambique - Papomo. Formed by *Adelino Gwambe*, in Malawi, but the Malawi Government objected to its pro-Chinese Communist element.

11. *União Nacional Africana de Rombézia* – African National Union of the Rombesia – Unar. Created in 1969 in Malawi, with the aim of obtaining, by peaceful means, through negotiation with the Portuguese Government, the independence of the region of Mozambique between the rivers Rovuma and Zambesi – to be called Rombesia. It was openly opposed to Frelimo, which is described as "Communist and racialist".